Musical Form

Allyn & Bacon, Inc.   *Boston, 1964*

Musical

Form

Robert E. Tyndall

Associate Professor of Music
Long Beach State College

Library of Congress Catalogue Card Number 64-17460

Printed in the United States of America

for Jean

without whose inspiration and help
this book would never have been written

Preface

THIS BOOK provides an introduction to the basic principles of musical form. All the common forms are described, and in addition, various musical compositions having atypical structures are discussed in sufficient detail to permit an understanding of diverse forms.

The book is organized according to various formal principles as observed in musical composition, rather than according to historical periods as such; but, where they are pertinent, observations about the historical development of certain forms are included. The music of our own century is not treated separately, contemporary applications of each form being included in the chapters where appropriate. This organization enables the reader to use the insight gained from the study of older examples of a form in his examination of contemporary music. More important, it shows that contemporary composers make use of techniques that are outgrowths of the practices of older composers.

As each form is studied, it is first described and then illustrated with clear examples from the literature. The examples in the book are drawn from a limited number of sources to facilitate the acquisition of complete scores, which is strongly recommended in any thorough study of the principles involved. Basic material is taken from Volume I of Beethoven's *Piano Sonatas*, the *French Suites* of Bach, and Volume I of Bach's *Well-tempered Clavier*. In addition, the *Seventh Symphony* of Beethoven and the *Octet for Wind Instruments* of Stravinsky are presented in their entirety. Each movement is analyzed where appropriate, and the complete works are discussed in Chapter VII, which is devoted to the form of complete pieces, an area often neglected in introductory books on form. Other compositions are used where necessary to obtain specimens of all the forms. Elements of the form are referred to by measure number, and the standard practice of numbering a movement from start to finish is followed, except that first and second endings share the same bar numbers. Since the Stravinsky *Octet* has frequent rehearsal numbers and is obtainable in only one edition, points in this score are located in relation to the rehearsal numbers.

At the end of each chapter other examples of the form discussed are listed for further study. These are chosen to present the form in a variety of performance media and historical styles, including wherever possible examples from our own century. A study of all, or part, of these examples, plus whatever others may be appropriate, is an absolute necessity in gaining an insight into composers' formal techniques. Composition in a particular form is another excellent means of gaining insight into the nature of that form. Moreover it induces the student to examine other composers' solutions to formal problems with keen interest.

One serious problem in the study of form in music is the lack of a clear and universally accepted terminology. With the exception of one aspect of fugue, this book uses the terms that are in common use. Alternative terms are explained in footnotes.

The author wishes to express his appreciation to Dr. Charles Becker and Dr. Leon Dallin of the Music Department of Long Beach State College, Long Beach, California, for their invaluable assistance in the writing of this book.

The author also wishes to express his appreciation to Mr. Nelson M. Jansky, Director of the Music Department of Allyn and Bacon, for his great assistance.

Robert E. Tyndall

Table of Contents

Illustrations

Musical Form

Introduction

MUSIC IS AN art that exists in time. A musical composition progresses along a logical path from start to finish and is heard a bit at a time, but its total effect is as great as if the listener were exposed to the entire work at once. This unity is the result of the clear and complete organization of the composition, which combines the series of separate sounds that the listener hears into a total effect. The result is an impact far greater than any series of unrelated sounds could have, however beautiful they might be. This book is an introduction to the techniques by which composers accomplish the organization and structuring of a musical composition, a task made difficult by the elusive nature of sound, the expressive medium of the art of music. This study is important not only for the composer but also for the performer, since an understanding of the design of a composition is essential to its performance. Before proceeding to a discussion of specific musical structures and an examination of them in the literature, it is well to consider the means that the composer may use to build and organize a composition.

A fundamental element in the structuring of a composition is the division of the work into a series of blocks or sections. These sections are separated in time, the primary dimension of music. All but the very shortest compositions consist of two or more sections, and the interrelationships between the material contained in these sections is a major factor in the organization of the work. Even a very extensive piece consists of only a few sections, each of which is necessarily quite large. These large sections will then be divided into smaller ones, which may also be subdivided. Composers prefer this means of organization to the stringing together of a large number of small sections which would result in the loss of any concise plan of organization. In very large compositions, the biggest divisions are called *movements*. These are separated in time by a silence or pause between them and are generally of a very unlike nature, so that the separate identity of each movement is clearly established.

A second basic facet of musical design is the use of the technique of contrast and return. Since the temporal nature of music allows the listener to hear only one area of a composition at a time, and since the listener must hear these areas in a definite, prearranged order, the composer may introduce material, move on to new and contrasting material, and then return to the material that was presented first. This creates the effect of motion and of a final return to the point of departure. This practice of bringing back previously presented material is constantly used in the creation of form in music. Thus a limited amount of basic material can be made to create a much longer work, resulting in an intensity of expression that could not be obtained if ideas were presented once and never referred to again. Ideas may return in their original form, or they may be transformed to present new aspects and hence new meanings.

The basic elements of music are the actual building materials that are manipulated to construct musical forms. The most important of these elements is melody, the first element of a composition to attract the listener's attention and the most expressive feature of a composition. Melody provides most of the raw material for a composition, and is central in importance to music of all periods and styles. The melodic material of a composition may vary in size from several three- or four-note motives to a series of extensive, lyrical melodies. A melody that is used several times in a composition and is a basic element in the construction of its form is called a *theme*. Compositions are remembered and identified by their themes, and the complete works of a composer are often catalogued by listing their themes, since the main themes of a composition are unique to that work. Second only to melody in importance is the element of key relationship, or *tonality*. Each work has a central or basic tonality and, unless the work is exceedingly short, a series of secondary tonalities. The most common tonal plan for a composition begins in the tonic key, modulates to a closely related key, modulates to more distantly related keys, and finally returns to the tonic key. From the fact that it starts in the tonic, moves away from it, and returns to it, this plan is called a *tonal arch*. Here again is illustrated the principle of departure and return. While some form of arch is the most common tonal design, many different designs are possible, and all can be used with success. Each one provides a feeling of motion, for the composer must never lose sight of the dynamic nature of the art of music. A few composers of this century have created musical forms that do not use tonality as a basic factor in their design. These are the work of the atonal composers, and a discussion of forms lacking tonal plans will follow in connection with an explanation of the twelve-tone technique. Any other elements which can be manipulated for purposes of formal design may also be used by the composer to create his structures. Included among these are the various textures and tone colors that can be achieved in the sounding medium, and also such characteristics as tempo and dynamics. Sudden changes or contrasts of such elements are very useful in helping to differentiate the various sections of a composition. Not only is each of these elements important in itself, but the interplay among them is a very important aspect of formal design.

When an artist starts to paint a painting, he begins by locating the important figures and objects on the canvas, thus creating the main structure of the picture. As the painting progresses, he can stand back and study the total design as often as he desires, thus keeping complete control of the form of the work. Only when this form is completely satisfactory does he fill in the smaller details. It is inconceivable that the painter should first complete a square inch in the lower lefthand corner and then add successive square inches until the canvas is full, since this technique would make it impossible to achieve any unity of design. In the same way, it is inconceivable to think of a composer composing a piece of music a measure at a time. Like the painter, the composer must start with the main outlines of the form of the work and then gradually fill in more and more detail until the piece is complete. Since he cannot actually step back and see the piece, he must look at it in his mind with the aid of his memory. In the study of musical form it is necessary to analyze in detail a large number of different types of pieces. This process is the reverse of that used by the composer, since the analyst takes the completed work and unravels it until the large outlines of the form appear. It is valuable for the composer or analyst, as well as for the painter, to concentrate on the large lines of organization. To do this, one starts by dividing a piece into its main sections which in turn are examined to see if any of them will divide further. This process is continued until all the sections of all sizes are found. Each section is then examined to see what it actually contains, and the material is compared to that contained in the other sections. This book contains a series of analyses of compositions which serve to illustrate this process, but these are a mere handful compared to the number of works that should be studied to obtain even a basic understanding of musical form.

While it is true that each composition has a formal design that is to some extent unique, certain general formal patterns are used again and again. These general patterns have acquired names such as *binary form, rondo form,* and *sonata form.* While the recognition of these general types is useful both to the composer and to the analyst, care must be taken not to confound the discovery and labeling of one of these types with a thorough analysis of a composition's structure. Each of these types is only a very general pattern, and the details of design are different for each piece. Since the majority of pieces make use of one of these patterns as a structural basis, much of the material in this volume deals with them. However, in the final chapter, pieces that do not conform to one of these types will also be considered, and it must be remembered that the presence or absence of one of the typical patterns in no way provides the basis for a critical evaluation of a composition. If a composition has two or more movements, these designs provide the basis for the structure of each individual movement. The structure of multimovement works will form the topic of a later chapter, but first consideration will be given to the form of single movements.

I

Phrase

Structure

THE PHRASE IS a small basic unit of musical structure. The probable origin of the phrase in the breath pauses necessary in vocal music makes it a very natural unit of structure, one common to all styles of music. The smallest musical structure, the *motive*, will be examined in Chapter III. Since motives may consist of as few as two notes, it is not possible to define a phrase as the smallest structural unit, a fact that greatly complicates the definition of the term. A phrase may be described as a small melodic unit capable of standing alone, but this definition is only satisfactory if it is realized that many phrases do not sound very conclusive and need a second phrase to make a complete thought. What constitutes a phrase can best be discovered from the examination of a number of phrases, and the examples in this chapter will provide a better definition of the term *phrase* than can be stated in words.

In all the examples in this chapter, the slurs used by the composers have been omitted, and instead long slurs have been used to indicate the duration of the phrases. This is necessary because composers do not generally mark their phrases, and there is no musical symbol that is commonly used for this purpose. If each of the phrases found in this chapter is studied carefully and sung or played, a clearer understanding of what constitutes a phrase will result.

PHRASE AND SENTENCE

A phrase is a melodic unit, and in a homophonic style the accompaniment may also be phrased to support the melodic structure. That is why, in Example 1, the slurs that indicate phrasing are applied only to the important melody. The harmony and the rhythm of the harmony have the same structure as the phrases, but it will be noted that at the end of the fourth measure, the new phrase starts an eighth note before the bar line, while the chord does not change until the bar line.

EXAMPLE 1: Beethoven: *Piano Sonata in C Minor, Op. 13* (Pathétique) — *2nd Movement*

An important factor in the harmonic support of the structure of these two phrases is the presence of two cadences, a half cadence at the end of the first phrase and an authentic cadence at the end of the second. In the traditional harmonic style, the end of a melodic phrase is nearly always supported by some sort of cadence. Thus any study of cadences is also a study of phrase endings. In other harmonic styles, phrase endings are also supported by cadences, and each harmonic style must be studied to determine the methods by which cadences are established. At the same time it must be observed that harmonic cadences are not imperative for the delineation of phrase endings, since monophonic music also contains phrases.

The other examples in this chapter deal only with the phrase structure of melodies, but the relation between melodic phrasing and harmonic support is generally the same. If possible, these other examples should be examined in context both to see the setting of the phrases employed by the composer and to study their general context in the music.

Example 1 contains not only two phrases, but a larger unit as well. The ending of the first phrase is not conclusive, requiring a second phrase to finish out the thought and provide a concluding sound. Thus the two phrases are joined in a larger structure known as a *sentence*. More rarely, two sentences may be joined to make a *double sentence*, as seen in Example 2. In this case, the composer has provided greater unity by having the two phrases of each sentence share common material.

EXAMPLE 2:   Tchaikovsky: *Symphony No. 5 in E Minor, Op. 64—2nd Movement*

Each of these examples is a theme from a piece, that is, a complete melody which is a basic idea used to build the form of the piece. This means that each of these melodies is meant to stand complete in itself. Not all sentences and phrases are so neatly constructed; the phrase structure is sometimes ambiguous, and phrases may not combine into sentences. A sentence may consist of more than two phrases. The one in Example 3 has three phrases, each one completely different from the others. This sentence opens the sonata and is followed by a two-phrase sentence to form a double sentence that serves as a theme.

EXAMPLE 3: Mozart: *Piano Sonata in F, K. 332—1st Movement*

A more unusual structure is found in Example 4, where a three-phrase sentence is followed by a repeat of the last two phrases of that sentence to form a second sentence and hence a double sentence of a most ingenious design.

EXAMPLE 4: Prokofiev: *Classical Symphony—Gavotte*

A sentence may occasionally be found that consists of four phrases, but usually four phrases form a double sentence of the type seen in Example 2. Some phrases can be further divided into halves called *sections*. However, this is not true of every phrase, which is a good reason for considering the phrase as the basic structural unit,

8   *Musical Form*

since it is the smallest unit that appears consistently. All of the phrases in the four previous examples consist of two sections. The next two examples, however, cannot be so subdivided.

PHRASE SIZE

All the phrases in the previous examples are four bars long, and this is the most usual phrase length. It should not be concluded that this represents the best or most expressive size for a phrase, but it is useful to have some concept of the general length of a phrase so that *phrase*, *section*, and *sentence* can be distinguished from one another. Other phrase sizes can be found; Examples 5 and 6 show phrases that are only three bars long.

EXAMPLE 5: Schubert: *Symphony No. 7 in C—2nd Movement*

EXAMPLE 6: Haydn: *Symphony No. 97 in C* (Solomon)*—1st Movement*

Example 7 shows a five-bar phrase, an exceedingly long one in view of the slow tempo. There are two sections, the first of which is two bars long and the second three bars.

EXAMPLE 7: Beethoven: *Piano Sonata in D, Op. 10, No. 3—2nd Movement*

In Example 8, a six-bar phrase is constructed of three two-bar sections, showing that a phrase may have two or three sections, just as a sentence may have two or three phrases. This makes a much greater variety of sizes and designs possible. Although the two-phrase sentence that consists of two four-bar phrases, each with two sections, is the most common, it is not the only possibility. As with any aspect of an art, the common structure may be "perfect," but if it is used consistently, the rhythm of the phrasing will become sing-song, predictable, and dull.

EXAMPLE 8:   Mozart: *Symphony No. 40 in G Minor, K. 550—3rd Movement*

Another technique contributing to the irregularity of phrase length is that of *phrase extension*. The melody in Example 9 starts with a four-bar phrase, and the answering phrase in this sentence would also have been four bars long had it ended on the first note of the eighth measure. Instead, the motion continues with a descending figure that is embellished and repeated an octave lower in the next bar. The F to E flat (the last note of bar 9 and first of bar 10) is repeated, leading to a full cadence which finally brings the phrase to an end, seven measures long instead of the expected four. Such an extension of the phrase increases the drama of the ending of the sentence and is an important factor in the expression of this melody.

EXAMPLE 9:   Beethoven: *Piano Sonata in B Flat, Op. 22—2nd Movement*

The melody from the scherzo of the Beethoven *Piano Sonata* found in Example 10 would seem, at first glance, to be an eight-bar phrase. However, when it is played at a fast tempo, one beat to the measure, the bars combine in pairs of one strong and one weak bar, and the effect on the listener is one of four two-beat bars. This gives the impression of a normal four-bar phrase, although the notation used shows eight bars. To further visualize this, imagine this example rewritten in six-eight time. It would then occupy the normal four bars.

EXAMPLE 10: Beethoven: *Piano Sonata in D, Op. 28—3rd Movement*

This is not to say that Beethoven could or should have written this scherzo in six-eight time. While the use of three-four time is probably historically a result of a speeding up of the minuet, the one-beat bar is very useful to composers. Six-eight time is necessarily a two-beat meter consisting of one strong and one weak beat. While a scherzo tends to use the one-beat bar to produce the same effect, the composer is under no obligation to do so. He may write a strong beat followed by one, two, or even three weak beats, or he may even use two or more strong beats in succession. An excellent example of this technique is the scherzo of the *Ninth Symphony*, in which Beethoven gives specific instructions that the meter is to consist in some places of groups of four bars and in other places of groups of three bars.

Another factor affecting the apparent length of phrases and sentences is the practice of using one bar as both the end of one phrase and the beginning of the next. This device, known as *elision*, may be seen in Example 11. The first four-bar phrase is combined with the next, which is also four bars long, to make a sentence. The D in the eighth bar of this example is clearly the end of that sentence. However, this eighth bar is also clearly the first bar of the next phrase, and carries the *fortissimo* dynamic of the new phrase.

Note that two of the slur marks touch this D, one ending on it, and one starting with it. With the use of elision, two four-bar phrases may be combined into a seven-bar sentence, one bar doing double duty. This is one more way in which the too regular effect of four-bar phrases can be alleviated.

EXAMPLE 11: Haydn: *Symphony No. 104 in D* (London)—*1st Movement*

FURTHER OBSERVATIONS ABOUT PHRASING

From Example 8 it is evident that a phrase can encompass short periods of silence with no loss of continuity. A more extreme example of this is seen in Example 12, where for two measures there is more silence than music, but where the complete four-bar phrase is heard as a unit. This is because the metrical beat continues in the listener's mind, so that the continuity of the phrase is not disturbed by the silence. It is very important to the phrasing of this example that the beat during the rests be steady.

EXAMPLE 12: Beethoven: *Piano Sonata in D, Op. 10, No. 3—Finale*

The previous dozen examples have been from music of a relatively homophonic texture, and the only phrasing considered was that of the main melody. If several melodies of equal importance are combined in polyphonic texture, it is possible that they will not always phrase at the same moment. Simultaneous breaks in the phrases are often avoided to create that continuous flow of musical sound that is so much a part of polyphony. In this case, all that has been said about phrase structure would be true, but the phrasing of each melody would have to be considered separately. Example 13 is a passage from the *Goldberg Variations* written out in open score (the original is in two lines for a keyboard instrument), with phrase marks applied to each part. The exact ending of some of the phrases is a bit vague, and the solution presented is a subjective one. But although someone else might arrive at a slightly different phrasing, anyone playing the piece would have to decide on some phrase structure. Finding and executing the phrases add immeasurably to the difficulty of playing this type of music.

EXAMPLE 13:   J. S. Bach: *Goldberg Variations—Variation 22*

An interesting example of a more extended nature is the theme of the *Haydn Variations* of Brahms shown in Example 14. The entire theme consists of three sentences of two phrases each, the first

and third of which have an obvious similarity of material. The first
sentence consists of two phrases, each five bars long, and the second
sentence of two four-bar phrases. The third sentence is composed of
two phrases that are five and seven bars long respectively, but the
two are elided so that the sentence totals only eleven bars. Each of
the variations that follow uses the same phrase and sentence structure, and the entire work should be heard and studied to see the
effect of the continued use of this very complex and unusual phrase
pattern. As a finale, Brahms wrote a set of variations over a ground
bass that is five bars long, taking this unusual length from three of
the phrases in his theme.

EXAMPLE 14:   Brahms: *Variations on a Theme of Haydn, Op. 56b*

All the examples in this chapter have shown a series of complete
phrases. However, such is not always the case in music, and an attempt to phrase an extensive piece will disclose places where inte-
gral phrases are not used and where the phrase structure is very
free. Such passages are difficult to demonstrate in short examples,
but their existence should be noted.

EXAMPLES FOR ANALYSIS

Almost any music can be profitably analyzed for phrase structure.
Since many of the examples in this chapter are from the first volume

of the *Piano Sonatas* of Beethoven, and since these are universally available, a number of movements are suggested here for introductory phrase analysis. Start each analysis at the beginning of the movement and look at a number of movements, at least in part, so that a variety of meters and tempos can be studied.

Sonata No. 1, Op. 2, No. 1—Slow Movement and *Finale*
Sonata No. 4, Op. 7—Slow Movement
Sonata No. 6, Op. 10, No. 2—1st Movement
Sonata No. 8, Op. 13—Finale
Sonata No. 9, Op. 14, No. 1—Allegretto (2nd Movement)
Sonata No. 12, Op. 26—Scherzo
Sonata No. 15, Op. 28—1st Movement, 2nd Movement, and
    Finale

The fugues of the *Well-tempered Clavier* of Bach furnish excellent material for the analysis of phrasing in polyphonic music.

II

Small Forms

THIS CHAPTER IS devoted to several specific musical designs which
may be spoken of as *forms*, since any one of them can be the general
form of a piece. The forms discussed in this chapter are called *small
forms* since they are relatively simple in design and are used for
rather short simple pieces. In later chapters forms of a more complex nature will be studied, which are referred to as *large forms*.
This designation is only relatively accurate, for a small form may be
the basis for a large movement, and a large form may be used in a
movement that is rather simple and quite short.

TERNARY FORM

The form of a piece of music is perceived by the listener in two
ways. The over-all structure is seen in the same way as the design of
a work of architecture or graphic art, and, since music is an art that
exists in time, the form is also seen in terms of movement. This

means that as a piece progresses the listener has a feeling of forward motion from familiar to new material, from section to section. The structure and balance of a piece of music is designed by the composer with these two viewpoints in mind. From either point of view, the ternary form is one of the simplest and most satisfying forms ever devised, one that centuries of use have not worn out.

As its name implies, a ternary form consists of three sections or parts. Each of these parts has sufficient unity and completeness to stand alone as a separate entity, and this easily perceived division into sections is a basic characteristic of the form.[1] Its other basic characteristic is that the first two sections are sufficiently different for each to have a separate identity, while the third section consists of a second statement of the material of the first section. This may be a literal return of all the music of the first section, sometimes not even written out for the player but rather played *da capo*. Sometimes this third section varies or transforms the material of the first section, but it is essential to the form that no transformation be made that conceals from the listener that the first and third parts are versions of the same section, and that the third part of the form consists not of new material but of familiar material returning. It is useful to give each of the sections of a form a label, and the convention has arisen to use letter names for this purpose. The first section encountered in a piece is called *Section A* and each new section is called successively *Section B, C,* and so on as needed. If a section found later in the piece seems essentially a return of an earlier section, the letter name of the earlier section is used each time it returns. This makes the customary letter designation of ternary form A B A. Such a description is very brief and graphic, but too much emphasis must not be put on these letter designations, lest the nature of the forms be oversimplified to the point where no real understanding of them results. One can imagine many different patterns of sections, but composers have actually used only a very few of the possibilities, suggesting that certain arrangements of sections make more satisfying and successful forms.

It is revealing that the three sections of ternary form are not three different sections, each of new material (A B C), but are rather two different sections, the first returning to make the third section (A B A). When the piece is viewed as a whole, the two outside sec-

[1] Each section can be said to stand alone in the sense that it is a complete, self-contained unit. In another sense, no section of a piece can stand alone, since all sections must be assembled to create the entire piece.

tions are alike and balance each other, at the same time framing the center section. If the form is perceived in terms of motion through time, it is evident that the listener hears the first section, moves next to a contrasting section, and finally returns to the original point of departure. Two basic elements of musical form are found here—the presentation of two sections that are contrasting, and the return in a later part of the piece of material that was first presented early in the work. This, together with the simple and direct nature of the form, accounts for its great popularity with composers; indeed, it seems as basic a form as can be found.

Another point worth noting is that ternary form is a structure that is too simple to be found in the other arts. Can you imagine a painting in which balance is achieved by having two figures, one on each side of the canvas, that are exact duplicates of one another? Or a three-stanza poem in which unity resulted from having the third stanza copy the first literally? Yet a ternary form in which the first two sections are written out and the third section is produced by a *da capo* of the first is just that literal and symmetrical a structure. Because the medium of music, abstract sounds, is the most obscure medium of any art, composers compensate by creating structures that are easy to perceive.

In the general description of the form given previously, it was stated that the A and B sections would be different from each other, but the nature of this difference was not mentioned. This is because composers use any means at their disposal to give each of these sections an identity. A basic and commonly used means is that of having a different theme in each section. Contrast of keys is another standard technique, and this is especially desirable since the third section will return the original key and a tonal arch will result. Actually these are but two of many techniques used to differentiate between the first two sections, and it is the variety of possible treatments that contributes to the long life of this form.

Beethoven: *Piano Sonata in F Minor, Op. 2, No. 1—2nd Movement*

This movement is a ternary form, the first 16 bars comprising the A section. This section is completely in the tonic key, F major. The section has two melodic ideas, the first beginning in bars 1, 5, and 13, and the second in bar 9. Section B starts in bar 17 and continues to the end of bar 31. The beginning of the B section establishes a new key, D minor, and a new theme, changing the whole mood of the movement, and contrasting strongly with the A section. Section B does not come to a complete close, but rather flows into a passage that prepares for the return of the opening of the A section in bar 32. This means that the end of the B section is apparent not because of a strong ending, but rather because of the return of the A section.[2] This is very common in ternary form, and it puts a double burden on the return of the A section. The moment of this return must be made very obvious to the listener since, if it passes unnoticed, the design of the piece and its effect are lost. This return also offers a very dramatic moment, and composers take advantage of its expressiveness. Bars 32 through 47 are a return of the entire A section, but in the interests of variety of expression Beethoven makes some changes, mostly in the embellishment of the melody. However, these in no way obscure the fact that this third section is a return of the entire first section. By bar 47 the form of the movement is complete, but Beethoven adds a short section to bring the movement to a close. Any such section that is added following the completion of the form is called a *coda*.

Beethoven: *Piano Sonata in F Minor, Op. 2, No. 1—Menuetto*

Beethoven made use of the ternary form twice in the writing of this movement. The minuet and trio are each ternary forms. We will first consider only the minuet (all that precedes the trio). Notice that while this is a ternary form, there are just two repeated strains.[3] This is a very common practice, and is due to the fact that the presence of repeated strains is rarely important to the form of a piece. The form is complete if no repeats are taken. If the performer should elect to take the repeats, the basic form is not changed, but rather some sections are heard more than once before the succeeding sections are heard. In this minuet, the first section (A) is found in the first strain and the other two sections (B A) are the second strain. The form is like the diagram in Example 15, and depending upon whether no repeats, either one, or both repeats were taken, the letter plans given represent the actual order in which the parts are heard. These are not considered as a number of different formal designs, but rather as one form, the different repeat patterns being heard as alternate ways of playing through or presenting the same form.

[2] See footnote, page 25.
[3] The term *strain* is commonly used to indicate a repeated section.

‖: A :‖: BA :‖ = A BA or A A BA or

A BA BA or A A BA BA

The tonic key of the minuet is F minor, and the first A section starts in that key. However, by the end of this section in bar 14, a modulation to the relative major key (A flat) has taken place. The B section starts from this key and proceeds to B flat minor, the subdominant, before returning to F minor in bar 29 for the beginning of the third section. Now, however, the A section must be changed to end in F minor, not in A flat major. In accomplishing this, Beethoven makes this A section two bars shorter than the first. Moreover, the beginning of A in bar 29 returns in the left hand instead of in the right. In spite of these changes, the passage from bar 29 on sounds like a return of the first section, not like a new section. When the A section is altered on its return, it is sometimes useful to designate it as altered by affixing a prime to the letter. Thus the form of this minuet could be called A B A'. A second return of a section which is further changed can be designated with a double prime. Since there is commonly some small change when a section is returned, it is difficult to say when there is enough change to justify the A' designation. In this minuet the B section makes use of no new melodic material, using instead fragments from the theme of A. This technique adds unity to the piece; however, the two parts can still be distinguished melodically, since section A presents the melodic material and section B develops fragments of it.

The trio is a very similar ternary form. The first strain, the A section, starts in the tonic key of the trio, F major, and modulates to the dominant key—C major. The B section, bars 51 to 65, stays largely in the tonic and is based on material from the A section. The third section is two bars shorter than the original A section and is altered to stay in the tonic key.

This movement offers a third example of ternary form, for since the *da capo* is always played, the resulting minuet – trio – minuet is in itself a ternary form. In this case the first and third sections are identical, as is always the case when the third section is created by directing the player to repeat the first section. Such a repetition is clearly an exception to the general statement that repeated sections do not affect the form, and for this reason, the *da capo* is not optional.

These examples serve to introduce ternary form. Clearly much variety is possible within the form, as can be gathered from the fact that each of these examples differs from the others. However, certain general observations can be made. The first and third sections may be identical or they may be quite different. The critical point in the third section is its beginning, since the start of the third section must at once suggest that we are not hearing a new section, but rather a previous section returning. But once this return has been clearly established, it is not necessary to continue a literal presentation of the original A section, and composers often make changes for tonal reasons and for variety. Great variety is also found in the content of the B section. The only valid statement possible is the one made earlier that B must somehow contrast with A and must also have enough that is characteristic to stand alone as a section. Typically B either introduces a new theme which contrasts with the theme of A and is its equal in importance, or has no new material but rather develops material from A.

Most ternary forms make use of a tonal arch, presenting at least one key other than tonic in the B section. Beyond this there are two varieties of the form, one which makes an initial modulation in the first A section, ending most commonly in the dominant key, and the other which ends the first A section in the tonic key and reserves any change of key for the B section. Obviously, in the former case, the return of the A section cannot be literal, since it must be changed at least enough to remain in the tonic key. Since the ternary form is small and simple, modulations tend to be to closely related keys. Even with this limitation composers prefer the dominant. The subdominant is rarely used early in a piece, composers evidently fearing that if the subdominant key is introduced before the tonic is securely established, it will tend to usurp the function of tonic, forcing the tonic key to sound like a dominant. The relative major is frequently the second key in pieces in the minor mode, but the use of relative minor in a work in major is much rarer. These observations about key structure apply not only to ternary form but to pieces in most forms.

A final aspect of the form to consider is the way in which the sections are separated. The first A section usually comes to a full close, and this makes the listener aware that one section has ended even before he hears the start of the next one. The B section makes no such stop, and it is often not evident that B has ended until the third section (the return of A) has started. This continuous flow from the second to the third section offers a logical explanation of why composers often write this form in two repeated strains. The return of A is a dramatic moment in a ternary form, but since it is not as effective on a second hearing, the second repeat in a long ternary form is often omitted by performers.

The temporal aspect of the art of music is well illustrated by considering just what liberties are possible in returning the A section of a ternary form. The critical issue is not what portion of the first and third sections are similar, but rather that the very beginning of the third section be instantly identified as the return of A. After this identification has taken place, the composer can take great liberties with the exactness of the return without losing the effect of the form. This is well illustrated by the minuet of the *Sixth French Suite* of Bach. Bar 17 is clearly the return of A in a ternary form, but in bar 19 the melody is greatly changed and what follows bears only a casual relationship to the first A section. An even more remarkable example is found in the minuet of Mozart's *Symphony No. 40 in G Minor*. In bar 28 the first violins play the first two bars of the melody of the A section, and in bar 29 the second violins enter imitating this same two-bar fragment. The alternation of this fragment continues, and the melody of A is never heard in its entirety, but because bar 28 sounds so completely like the start of the return of the A section, the effect of a ternary form is clearly achieved. Another example of extreme alternation of the return is found in Mozart's next symphony, the *Jupiter Symphony*. The success of the effect in this case is largely due to the return of the tonic key at the start of the third section.

BINARY FORM

As its name implies, a binary form consists of two parts. This would seem to be a simpler form than ternary, but such is not the case, and some binary forms are very subtle and difficult to analyze. This complexity is the result of two factors. In the first place, composers are loath to make the two sections completely unrelated, since this would mean introducing several new themes which would never be returned. Instead, the material in the B section is generally drawn in part or completely from the material in the A section, and there is often little thematic separation between the two sections. Secondly, the A section rarely ends in the tonic key, so that the tonal arch begins in the A section and must end in the B section since there is no third section in which the tonic can be returned. This means that the tonic key does not return at an important juncture of the form, but enters, often rather subtly, in the middle of a section. The departure from or return to the tonic can be of no assistance in differentiating the parts of the form. This leaves the break between the two parts as the most important means of identifying the two sections, and it is customary in binary form to begin and end each section clearly. If repeats are used they are placed so that each part is repeated separately, making the form with repeats sound like A A B B.

J. S. Bach: *French Suite No. 5 in G Major—Allemande*

This is a binary form in which the two parts are symmetric. Each part is 12 bars long, each starts with the same melody, and each ends with the same melody. Much of the differentiation of the two parts depends on the key pattern. The movement starts with the tonic key of G major and midway through the A section modulates to the dominant key, D major. The B section starts in that key and passes through tonic to the relative, E minor, returning from that key to the tonic in bar 19. This means that although the same melody starts both parts, it is in G major at the beginning of the A section and in D major at the beginning of the B section. Likewise, the melody that ends both sections is found in D major at the end of the A section and in G major at the end of the B section. Clearly, key center is an important means of differentiating these themes in the two sections. The entire B section contains material derived from the A section, and a thorough analysis will reveal many subtle changes and treatments of this material.

J. S. Bach: *French Suite No. 5 in G Major—Gavotte*

This gavotte is a less symmetrical binary form, the A section being eight bars long and the B section exactly twice as long. This is often the case, and if the two halves of a binary form are not equal in length, B is the longer section, possibly because the tonal arch reaches its most distant point in the early part of the B section. The key pattern of the gavotte is the same as that for the movement just discussed, G – D – E minor – G. Here there is more melodic separation, since the figure that starts the second part is the inversion of the figure that starts the first part. The phrase that starts midway in bar 20 is remarkably like the very opening of the A section, and while this does not really make the gavotte a ternary form, it does at least hint at a return of the A section material late in the second part.

The gigue of the *French Suite* from which these two movements were taken illustrates a complete melodic separation of the two parts of the form, the theme of the B section being the inverted form of the theme of the A section.

DISTINGUISHING BINARY AND TERNARY FORM

It would seem a simple matter to tell if a piece is in binary or ternary form, but such is not the case. In the discussion of ternary form it was seen how little of the first A section must be returned to make a ternary form, and in the discussion of binary form, it was noted that there is sometimes a hint of a return of the opening late in the B section. The problem of assigning one form or the other to a piece is sometimes vexing and causes great difficulty in spite of the seemingly simple nature of the two forms discussed. The consideration of a specific example will illustrate this. The minuet of *Eine Kleine Nachtmusik* of Mozart is a seemingly simple, straightforward movement consisting of two eight-bar repeated strains. But if one considers the phrase structure of the melody and identifies the phrases, the following relationship becomes evident:

EXAMPLE 16:   Mozart: *Eine Kleine Nachtmusik—3rd Movement*

The second phrase of the first part is a variant of the first phrase and is therefore identified as *a'*. The first phrase of the second part is completely different and is labeled *b*, but the last phrase is a literal return of the second phrase and is also labeled *a'*. At first glance this would seem to be a binary form, since the two parts are exactly the same size and end with the same material. This is the same procedure as that found in the Bach allemande. But the matter does not stop here, for the phrase that is used to end both sections is very similar to the first phrase of the first section, and when *a'* returns after the clear digression of *b*, the effect is of a ternary form. This could easily be the case because the return of the A section in a ternary form need be neither literal nor of the same length as the original section. Even the repeat structure is of no assistance in this classification, since both ternary and binary forms are commonly found with two repeated strains. The dilemma is caused not by this piece, which is really very simple, but by the basic premise that binary and ternary are two completely different forms, and that a small piece such as this must be in either one form or the other. It would be more realistic to view binary and ternary forms as opposite poles of a continuum. A form such as this one should be placed on this continuum at a point approximately half-way between the poles. A dogmatic statement that this movement is a binary form or a ternary form does little to describe the actual structure of the piece, although it does make for some lively controversy. The problem of assigning certain pieces to either the binary or ternary category has long vexed theorists, and it seems in part a product of the faulty concept that binary and ternary forms are separate entities. At best, the matter is not a simple one, but it is from such vexing variety that these two forms take their vitality.[4]

[4] With respect to specific works under study, musical scholars have not always agreed as to how the concept of ternary form should be applied. One view, rather rigid in its philosophy, considers a ternary form to exist only if the first and third sections are identical and if the first section ends with a conclusive cadence in the tonic key. Differing in some respects where specific application is concerned is the widely held view that considers any movement in three basic sections, in which the third section is essentially a return of the first, to be in ternary form. The author holds to this view, which is represented in the analyses on these pages. The examples used and the explanations concerning them permit an understanding of the basic characteristics of the form under discussion, and will be quite clear to the reader and student.

COMPOUND TERNARY FORM

Although the binary and ternary forms studied so far were used for entire movements, another important use of these forms is as the design for a part of a larger movement. We have already touched on this usage in discussing the minuet and trio from Beethoven's *Piano Sonata in F Minor, Op. 2, No. 1.* Taken as a whole the movement is a ternary form (minuet – trio – minuet) of the most literal kind, the first and third sections being exact duplicates of each other. Each of the sections of this large form is, in turn, a ternary form, and this use of small forms to construct the three parts of a large ternary form is termed a *compound ternary form.*[5] This use of the same form for both the design of the whole movement and the design of its component parts leads to considerable confusion in discussing the form of the movement, unless it is made clear exactly which form is being considered at the moment. In describing the form of this movement in letters, upper and lower case letters are valuable to differentiate between the various levels of form. Example 17 is a diagram of a compound ternary form in which the large parts are each also ternary forms.

EXAMPLE 17:   Diagram of a Compound Ternary Form

Minuet	Trio	Minuet
A	B	A
a b a	c d c	a b a

The two different sections of the trio are called *c* and *d* to show that they differ from the corresponding sections of the minuet. Sometimes in a compound ternary form one or both of the large sections is a binary instead of a ternary form. The following example illustrates this.

[5] This form is also known as *Song Form* and *Minuet and Trio Form.* Both these terms have the disadvantage of naming the form for one application. Actually, this is not a new form but a new use of ternary form, and the above-used name is based on that fact.

Beethoven: *Piano Sonata in C Sharp Minor, Op. 27, No. 2*
        (Moonlight)—2nd Movement

This scherzo is a compound ternary form in which the first and third sections (scherzo) are in ternary form, and the second section (trio) is in binary form. We will consider first the ternary form of the first scherzo. Part A is eight bars long, and is repeated in the next eight bars. This repeat is written out so that this section can be varied by adding suspensions. It is not uncommon for composers to write out the repeat of a strain either to change the scoring or the setting or to actually vary the music, as is the case here. These repeats are harder to detect than those marked with repeat signs, but they have no more effect on the form than any other repeated strain. Obviously when a repeat is written out the performer cannot elect to omit it. Notice here that Beethoven takes the precaution of instructing the pianist not to repeat the first strain, lest the A section be heard four times instead of the intended two. Section B follows from bars 17 to 24, and in bar 25 section A returns, extended from eight to twelve measures by a more conclusive ending. This is logical, since bar 36 not only ends the scherzo section of the movement, but on the *da capo* will end the movement as well. The trio is a binary form, and in a wonderful touch Beethoven uses many anticipations in the trio, as he had used many suspensions in the scherzo. The key pattern in this movement is unusual in that both the scherzo and trio are in D flat and neither really leaves that key.

A further development of this form is the use of two trios in a minuet or a scherzo. Each trio is complete, but the two are different from each other, and the movement is played scherzo – trio I – scherzo – trio II – scherzo. This puts considerable burden on the scherzo, since it will be heard three times instead of the usual two. This form bears a certain resemblance to rondo form, as will be seen when that form is studied, but it is merely an extension of compound ternary form and is used in movements where compound ternary form is usually found. In several of his symphonies, Beethoven used a further varient of compound ternary form in which the scherzo is played three times and the trio is played twice. The succession of parts is like the form with two trios described previously, but a single trio is used, which is heard twice. In the *Seventh Symphony* Beethoven uses a notable refinement of this form that is worth studying.

Beethoven: *Symphony No. 7 in A, Op. 92—3rd Movement*

The scherzo and trio (*Presto* and *Assai meno presto*) are both ternary forms, and should be analyzed before the whole movement is studied. One unusual feature of the scherzo is worth noting. In bar 64 there is a false return of the A section of the ternary form, the opening theme occuring in the oboe in the key of B flat, the subdominant. The true return comes a few measures later in bar 89. This oboe solo is so effective that it is interesting to speculate whether Beethoven wished to use the main theme in the oboe, and finding that it did not lie well for that instrument in the tonic key of F, made the B flat false return in order to have a range which was effective for the oboe. Another unusual feature of this movement is the key relationship between scherzo and trio, F major and D major, which results in a cross relation between F natural and F sharp. The most important feature of this movement, and one of the true masterstrokes of formal design, results from Beethoven's desire to avoid the monotony that might result from three literal appearances of the scherzo. In the second appearance of the scherzo he achieves the effect of an echo by marking the music *sempre p*, without changing the scoring. Played well this is one of the great effects in the literature. For the third appearance of the scherzo, the original dynamics return, so that the echo form of the scherzo is framed by the two normal versions.

The compound ternary form is not a new form as such, but rather a new principle of using two forms already studied. Before leaving this form, mention should be made of a special outgrowth of this form—the *Street March* of the type commonly played by bands. Originally the form of these marches must have followed the pattern of the compound ternary form, but it has long been customary to omit the *da capo* and end with the trio. Most marches played today were written after this practice developed and were intended by their composers to be played this way. The typical march has a short introduction followed by a first part which is usually in binary form. There follows a trio in the subdominant which may be either binary or ternary form. This trio takes on greater importance since it is to end the piece, and if there is one melody in the march which dominates all the others, it is usually found in the trio. This form is unusual both in that the trio is more important than the first section and in that the work ends in a key other than the one in which it started. The key of the first section and that of the trio seem of equal importance, a technique rarely used in music.

RONDO FORM

The significant characteristic of rondo form is that the principal theme, or *rondo theme*, occurs at least three times. This main theme is presented in the first section of the piece, and this section recurs at least two more times. In this way it differs from ternary form, in which the opening section returns but once. Between the appearances of this rondo theme section come other sections known as *episodes*, which present new thematic material and new key centers. Expressed in letters, the basic form of a rondo would be A B A C A, the rondo theme (section A) starting and ending the work and the successive episodes being each different. Rondo form may be longer than this if more episodes are used, but each new episode always comes between two appearances of the rondo theme section. Thus a rondo could take a form such as A B A C A D A or A B C A D A E A.[6]

In the second half of the eighteenth century the newly developed sonata form had an influence upon rondo that resulted in some alterations in the episode patterns. These will be studied later as *sonata-rondo* form. The standard key pattern of the rondo form before the twentieth century is that each appearance of the rondo theme is in the tonic key and the intervening episodes are in other keys, earlier episodes generally being in the more closely related keys. In this respect the rondo is unlike most other forms, since there is no large tonal arch extending throughout the piece. In contemporary music all the appearances of the rondo theme may not be in the tonic key, but they are still recognizable.

This form is essentially one in which material is presented rather than developed, and therefore composers have favored it for light gay finales of multimovement works. This practice leads to the misconception that the form is somehow limited to movements of this nature, although such is far from the truth. Indeed, none of the

---

[6] Some authorities further classify rondo forms according to their length, in these two cases noting that there are seven and nine parts instead of the usual five.

forms studied is dependent upon a particular mood for its nature; any one can be used successfully for many different sorts of movements. Rondos exhibit great variety in the method of connection of successive sections. In some rondos each section ends with a complete halt and the next section starts afresh, while in others the flow from one section to another is as smooth as would be found in any other form.[7]

Beethoven: *Piano Sonata in C Minor, Op. 13*
(Pathétique)—2nd Movement

A basic problem for the composer of a rondo form is that the rondo theme may pall during its many appearances. To avoid this, the composer writes a particularly engaging melody for his rondo theme, and this, in turn, contributes to the importance of the theme in the work. In this slow movement, Beethoven uses one of his typical broad, singing adagio themes as a rondo theme. The first 16 bars of the movement present the eight-bar rondo theme and a repetition of it. The first episode starts in bar 17 in the key of F minor (the relative), but modulates to the dominant key of E flat by bar 22. The last three bars of this episode lead back to the tonic key and in bar 29 the key of A flat and the rondo theme return simultaneously. Although this section is shorter than the first one, the rondo theme being heard only once, the familiarity of the material creates a balance between the first and third sections. The second episode starts in bar 37 and presents its theme in two different keys, first the tonic minor, and then the major key a third lower, E major (F flat major). Bars 48 through 50 modulate back to A flat, and in bar 51 the rondo theme returns for the last time. It is played and repeated as it was first heard, but in the interest of variety the accompaniment is changed to reflect the triplet rhythm first found in the second episode. From bar 67 to the end there is a short coda which brings the movement to a close by gradually slowing the motion.

[7] The type of connection of sections is likewise used as a further means of subdividing rondo forms. As before, it seems preferable to use *rondo* as the name of a general type of form and note the details of construction in an analysis of an individual rondo.

Stravinsky: *Octet—Finale*

The more complex version of rondo form mentioned earlier as *sonata-rondo* has not survived into this century, and today composers are again using the older simpler version of the rondo. The final movement of Stravinsky's *Octet* is in the form A B A C A with a coda. The movement starts with the rondo theme in the first bassoon in the key of C major. The theme is repeated two bars before number 58 with an obbligato part in the clarinet. The loud brass entrance at 61 announces the beginning of the first episode, and the main theme of this episode is heard in the second trumpet in the key of F. Three bars later a second part of this theme is heard, after which the second trumpet returns with the opening of the theme. A transitional passage leads to the return of the rondo theme in the fifth bar of 62. The rondo theme is exactly like the previous statement in the second bar before 58. At 65 the theme and its accompaniment are taken over by the two trumpets, and the key moves up a half step to D flat major. The second episode starts at 66 in the key of A flat with a theme in the flute, which is then varied by the first trumpet, trombone, and clarinet at number 67. By adding eighth notes to the characteristic syncopated motion of this theme, Stravinsky gradually increases the excitement. With no decrease of rhythmic motion and no feeling of a junction with a new section, the rondo theme suddenly appears in the first trombone part at number 69. Although the rhythm of the melody is changed, there is no doubt that it is the rondo theme and thus the start of the last section. The key is again C. At 70 the second trumpet takes the melody, after which the head of the melody is played several times as the motion gradually approaches a climax. However, at number 73 a sudden silence interrupts the expected climax, and there follows a coda based on the syncopated rhythm of the second episode.

The practice of varying the rondo theme as it recurs, found in both movements just discussed, is a common one and is sometimes carried to such extremes that if the successive rondo theme sections were removed from the piece and placed successively, a virtual theme and variations would result. The Finale of Beethoven's *Piano Sonata, Op. 79,* offers a good example of such a treatment of the theme. As it is first presented, the rondo theme is a small binary form quoted in two repeated strains. Here is one more example of a small form being used to construct a section of a large form, and here too is an example of a binary form in which sections A and B are not thematically related. When the rondo theme first returns, the quarter-note motion of its accompaniment is replaced with triplets, and both repeats are omitted. On the last appearance of the rondo theme, the accompaniment motion is further speeded up to sixteenth notes. In addition, each strain is again repeated, but the repeat is written out and the melody and accompaniment are embellished. Notice how much this gradual increase of excitement contributes to the forward flow of the movement.

EXAMPLES FOR ANALYSIS

TERNARY FORM

Beethoven: *Piano Sonata No. 12, Op. 26—1st Movement:* theme for the variations

Beethoven: *Piano Sonata No. 25, Op. 79—2nd Movement*

Bach: *Sixth French Suite—Menuet*

BINARY FORM

Bach: *Fifth French Suite.* All the movements of this suite are in binary form, and a study of them will reveal many variants of design. The gigue is very nearly in the form of a fugue as well.

The other *French Suites* also offer many binary forms, as do many other suite movements from the Baroque Era. A good source of binary forms in the music of the Classic and Romantic Eras is in the themes from theme-and-variation forms. The slow movement of Beethoven's *Piano Sonata No. 10, Op. 14, No. 2,* is a theme and variations. The theme should be analyzed in the light of the discussion of the form of the minuet from *Eine Kleine Nachtmusik* of Mozart.

COMPOUND TERNARY FORM

The minuets and scherzos of the Beethoven *Piano Sonatas* offer examples of this form. In some cases the subdivisions are ternary forms and in some cases binary. This form is often used for slow movements, two of which are:

Beethoven: *Piano Sonata No. 12, Op. 26—Marcia Funèbre*

Beethoven: *Piano Sonata No. 15, Op. 28—2nd Movement*

Many of the numerous short piano pieces of the Romantic Era make use of ternary or compound ternary form. Such pieces by Chopin, Schubert, Schumann, Brahms, and others are an excellent source of examples of all kinds of ternary forms.

RONDO

Beethoven: *Piano Sonata No. 25, Op. 79—Finale*

Bach: *Partita No. 3 for Violin Solo—Gavotte en Rondeau*

Haydn: *Piano Sonata in A Flat—Finale* (No. 41 in the Peters Edition)

Bartók: *Rondo No. 1 on Folk Tunes, Op. 6, No. 2*

III

The Motive

THE MOTIVE IS the smallest unit of musical form. Although it may consist of as few as two notes, a motive is always complete in itself and capable of standing alone. Motives are used as building blocks for larger elements of music, to construct a melody or to add unity to an extensive composition. However extensively motives are used, a primary reason for their use is the unity that they bring to a musical structure. After a motive has been introduced, it may either be used rather literally or extensively transformed. As in the case of phrases, a definition of motive and discussion of its use and transformation is easier in music than in words, and the examples in this chapter will provide such a definition.

Example 18, from a Haydn minuet, is based on a single motive, indicated by the bracket. The second appearance of the motive is essentially like the first at a lower pitch. For its third appearance the motive is altered. The four sixteenth notes descend in a scale line and the final repeated quarter notes are replaced by ascending eighth notes. The second phrase offers further variants of the motive; first the quarter notes are higher than the sixteenth notes and then the descending sixteenth-note pattern is combined with the quarter notes instead of with the eighth notes. Both phrases of this sentence end with the same variant of the motive.

EXAMPLE 18: Haydn: *Symphony No. 100 in G* (Military)—*3rd Movement*

In this example the motive is continuously present, but Example 19 shows a melody from a Brahms song in which the first and last notes are not motivic. If a motive is used to organize a melody, it is not necessarily continuously present, and may be present less than half the time.

EXAMPLE 19: Brahms: *Vergebliches Standchen, Op. 84, No. 4*

Example 20 is from a later portion of the same song, and here a second motive is introduced. The original motive is labeled *a* in Examples 19 and 20, and the new motive is labeled *b*. Notice the variant forms of motive *a* that are present.

EXAMPLE 20

If more than two motives are used it is difficult for any one motive to be repeated often enough to contribute much to the unity of the melody. For this reason a single motive is most commonly used, two different motives are less common, and more than two are used only rarely.

Motives have been seen so far in the construction of melodies, but they may also be used in more elaborate ways to unify entire passages, as the next two examples from a Bach fugue demonstrate. Example 21 is analyzed as containing two motives, although it will be seen that both motives have the same rhythm, a point demonstrated by Bach in the fifth bar, when both motives occur together. In a sense, then, there is only one basic motivic idea, and the motives labeled *a* and *b* are different versions of that motive. In this light the passage appears exceedingly tightly constructed.

EXAMPLE 21:   J. S. Bach: *Well–tempered Clavier, Vol. II—Fugue No. 5 in D*

Example 22 is an even more intensely unified passage from the same composition. Here each part is based almost exclusively on motive *b*, which is found a total of thirteen times in the course of only four measures.

EXAMPLE 22

In both these examples the value of motivic construction to achieve an interrelationship between contrapuntal parts is evident. The motives in the last example were used literally, but in the preceding examples they were transformed in many ways to avoid the monotony of too much literal repetition of motives. The transformations of motives are as varied as a composer's imagination can make them, the only limitation being that the various forms of the motive must bear enough relationship to the original form to be felt by the listener; otherwise, the variant forms of the motive will sound like new motives and contribute little to the unity of the piece. The first three appearances of the motive in Example 23 are actually literal repetitions of the motive, but since this device is of limited expressive value, Mozart then uses the motive three more times at new pitches.

EXAMPLE 23: Mozart: *Symphony No. 40 in G Minor, K. 550—1st Movement*

Motivic unity comes not from a literal repetition of the motive, which is easy to do but soon becomes dull, but rather from intensive use of a motive which is so constantly transformed that there is variety. The very presence of the motive gives unity, and the transformations of the motive prevent tedium.

The motives discussed in Examples 21 and 22 are used almost continuously to give unity to the fugue. This fugue and the other examples suggested at the end of the chapter should be studied to see the effect of a tightly knit motivic construction.

In a multimovement work, a motive will most often be found in a single movement, but sometimes two or more movements are unified by sharing a basic motive. The first movement of the *Fifth Symphony* of Beethoven starts with a two-bar motive which dominates the first movement, being present most of the time. To further unify the symphony, Beethoven uses this same motive—three short notes followed by a long note—for one theme in each of the other movements. These can be seen in Example 24. It should be noted that while all forms of the motive preserve the four-note relationship, the meter varies so that the accent pattern is not consistent. Sometimes the first of the three short notes is the strongest, sometimes the second. This does not obscure the identity of the motive, but it does introduce another degree of variety of its treatment which is necessary if the motive, which has been used exhaustively in the first movement, is to appear in other movements.

EXAMPLE 24:   Beethoven: *Symphony No. 5 in C Minor, Op. 67*

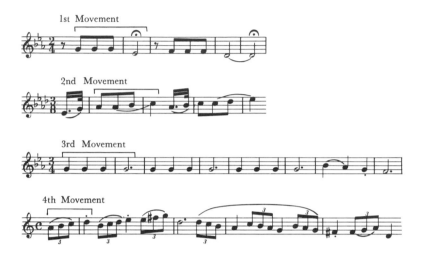

Although the use of one or more motives is a valuable device which helps the composer achieve unity within a melody, a phrase or section of a piece, a movement, or even an entire large composition, not all music employs motives. Many exceedingly expressive passages in music contain no discernable motives, and the presence or absence of a motive is no indication of the quality or expressiveness of a composition. Motivic structure exists in addition to those larger aspects of form that have been and will be studied. One ternary form could be composed that exhibited a high degree of motivic unity in its themes; another could be composed that made no use of motivic construction. Both pieces would be equally identifiable as ternary forms, and indeed, might well be identical in every other aspect of form. However, an analysis of the first piece would have to consider the motive structure, since the unity and thematic relationships contributed by it would be important to the piece. Moreover, motivic structure does make one important contribution to form in that it is an indispensable factor in the process known as *development*.

DEVELOPMENT

The sections within a piece of music may be divided into two very basic types—those which are essentially engaged in the presentation of material, and those that are engaged in developing material that has been previously presented. The process of development consists of taking a musical idea previously presented and varying it and altering its treatment to create a new passage. A very basic factor in this technique is that of drawing from a previous melody a basic motive and creating a new passage, often extensive, dominated by this motive. The typical uses of the technique of development will be discussed when the appropriate forms are studied, but it is desirable now to consider this process as it applies to motives, for it is one of their most important uses.

Example 25 is a theme from the first movement of a Beethoven piano sonata as it is quoted in the beginning of the passage devoted to its development.

EXAMPLE 25: Beethoven: *Piano Sonata in D, Op. 28—1st Movement*

From this melody Beethoven takes the last four measures as a motive and adds a counterpoint of eighth notes below it (Example 26).

EXAMPLE 26

Example 27, which follows closely, inverts the two lines of the previous example.

EXAMPLE 27

Beethoven next proceeds to a further fragmentation of the motive, using first two bars of it (Example 28), and then using a single bar (Example 29).

EXAMPLE 28

EXAMPLE 29

In this last form the motive is kept in the right hand and the eighth notes remain in the left hand. Example 30 shows a new form which discards the eighth notes so that the motive can appear in both hands. The form of the motive in the right hand, using a quarter rest followed by a quarter note, supplies a strong note on the second beat of each measure which creates rhythmic excitement after so much use of the original form of the motive, in which only the first beat of each measure was accented.

EXAMPLE 30

Example 31, which is a variant of Example 30, shows the final treatment of the motive in this extensive passage.

EXAMPLE 31

These examples can be seen in context in the middle part of the first movement of this sonata. Beethoven carefully shows the listener each step in his development of the theme, first quoting the theme, next selecting a long motive from it, then developing first this form and then successively shorter segments. Near the end of this movement one more development of this theme takes place, as shown in Example 32. Beethoven reiterates the last two bars of the theme preceded by a quarter-note pick-up, and this pick-up note becomes successively higher each time the figure is repeated, until all that is left is the quarter note, which is heard three times alone before the last chord.

EXAMPLE 32

An infinite number of varied treatments of a motive are possible in this process of development, and few places in a composition show off a composer's imagination to better advantage. Although the great variety of these procedures makes a survey of them impossible, one more set of examples will show further possibilities. These examples come from a Bach fugue, and, like the previous examples of Beethoven, are small samples of developments found throughout the work. The first occurrence of the motives developed is shown in Example 33. In the Beethoven example the motive

EXAMPLE 33: J. S. Bach: *Well-tempered Clavier, Vol. I—Fugue No. 12 in F Minor*

became successively shorter, but in this fugue the motive grows both in size and in elaborateness of treatment.

In Example 34 two voices use the motive in an inverted form and in Example 35 the order of the parts is changed.

EXAMPLE 34

EXAMPLE 35

The motive form in the top voice in Example 36 uses a longer string of sixteenth notes, as do the forms of the motive in Example 37.

EXAMPLE 36

Example 38 shows the last step in this development, using all the forms seen before, and using four voices for the first time.

EXAMPLE 37

EXAMPLE 38

An important element in both of these extensive developmental passages is the logical sequence of events. Each new treatment of the motive is similar to the last treatment, but a succession of changes brings us to a treatment that is startlingly new. The composer unfolds his plan of varying the motive a step at a time for the listener, being always careful that each new use of the motive is understood before proceeding on to the next. This is a process that is very basic to an art which exists in time, since it creates a continual feeling of forward movement.

MOTIVES THAT ARE ONLY PITCHES

The motives we have seen were short melodies, and as such had both pitches and rhythms. Of these two elements, rhythm was probably the more important of the two, and the one most basic in establishing the relationship between the variants of a motive. There is another class of motives—those that have only the attribute of pitch. These are not found in short segments of melody, but rather furnish the basic motivic ideas for large expanses of a composition or a complete work. Such a motive is Example 39, which dominates the entire *Second Symphony* of Brahms. The motive is shown here in whole notes to suggest rhythmless pitches, but clearly whenever Brahms uses it in the symphony he must give it some rhythm as well, so that it can be played in its proper place. The "rhythmless" aspect of the motive arises from the lack of any consistent rhythmic pattern, and also from the fact that its rhythmic pattern at the moment plays no part in the identification of the motive.

EXAMPLE 39

Example 40 shows the motive as it is heard in the first bar of the first movement, and Examples 41, 42, and 43 show three melodies from this movement that make use of the motive.

EXAMPLE 40:   Brahms: *Symphony No. 2 in D, Op. 73—1st Movement*

EXAMPLE 41

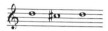

EXAMPLE 42

EXAMPLE 43

If a single motive is to dominate an entire symphony, the composer must do more than simply repeat it, and the technique shown here of using the motive to create a new melody is a useful one. Example 44 shows the inversion of the motive, this time used in a melody in the third movement.

EXAMPLE 44: Brahms: *Symphony No. 2 in D, Op. 73—3rd Movement*

This melody is, in turn, varied within the movement (Example 45), thus carrying the developmental process a step further.

EXAMPLE 45

Finally, in Example 46 the motive is shown as it is used to generate the main theme of the last movement.

EXAMPLE 46: Brahms: *Symphony No. 2 in D, Op. 73—Final Movement*

Beethoven uses a similar technique to connect three of his late string quartets. Example 47 shows the motive as it is presented in the first two bars of the first of the three quartets. In spite of its definite rhythm here, this too is a motive which consists only of pitches.

Example 48 is from the next movement of the same quartet. Here only the first three notes are used, and the sixth has given way to a third, the inversion of the interval.

EXAMPLE 48: Beethoven: *String Quartet in A Minor, Op. 132—2nd Movement*

Example 49 is the opening of the second quartet in the series.[1] Here the motive is included in a longer melody, and the minor second at the beginning moves down instead of up.

EXAMPLE 49: Beethoven: *String Quartet in B Flat, Op. 130—1st Movement*

Example 50, from the same movement, uses only the last three notes of the motive.

EXAMPLE 50

The last quartet in the series is represented by the next two examples, Example 51 coming from the beginning of the first move-

---

[1] These quartets were not written in the order indicated by their opus numbers, but rather in the order discussed in this book.

ment. Here the two minor seconds in the motive are each in their original direction, but the interval of a sixth has again been inverted to a third.

EXAMPLE 51:   Beethoven: *String Quartet in C Sharp Minor, Op. 131—1st Movement*

In Example 52, Beethoven actually uses the motive in retrograde, a relationship we will see frequently in the discussion of twelve-tone music.

EXAMPLE 52:   Beethoven: *String Quartet in C Sharp Minor, Op. 131— Last Movement*

The two twentieth-century compositions which are next discussed both use basic motives that are longer than those seen before. These may be considered both as motives and as basic scale forms. In each work the basic motive generates many passages, but the notes of the motive are not always used in order, and the motive is not always complete in any one passage. Yet in both compositions there does seem to be a basic motivic idea that generates the work in the same sense that the motives just seen generated the works by Brahms and Beethoven. The lack of precision found here in the description of the motives in these contemporary pieces is due to the difficulty of clearly perceiving the techniques of one's own era.

EXAMPLE 53

The basic motive for the Bartók *Fifth Quartet* is seen in Example 53, and Example 54 shows the opening theme of the quartet as growing out of this motive.

EXAMPLE 54: Bartók: *Fifth String Quartet—1st Movement*

Example 55 shows this same motive in an inverted form, and Example 56 is the same transposed up a tritone, in which form the motive generates Example 57, the first theme of the last movement.

EXAMPLE 55

EXAMPLE 56

EXAMPLE 57: Bartók: *Fifth String Quartet—Finale*

In the same way, the basic motive of Stravinsky's *Symphony in Three Movements*, seen in Example 58, generates the melody which is used for a fugue in the last movement.

EXAMPLE 58

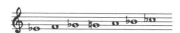

The Motive   49

The fugue melody is shown in Example 59 as it is first played by the piano.

EXAMPLE 59:   Stravinsky: *Symphony in Three Movements—Finale*

The first melody shown is from the last movement because it is here that the generating motive is most clearly seen, and this explains why the fugue seems to sum up the entire symphony. Example 60 is the same motive starting from the note F, in which form it accounts for every note of the first three bars of the symphony, shown in Example 61.

EXAMPLE 60

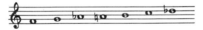

EXAMPLE 61:   Stravinsky: *Symphony in Three Movements—1st Movement*

These are only samples of the many uses of the motive found in these two works. One more example from Stravinsky's symphony should help to clarify this process. In Example 63, from the first movement, Stravinsky uses the basic motive starting on the note C, as shown in Example 62. He has altered the second note from D to D flat, and omits the G altogether, but notice that he ends with an F sharp followed by an A flat, the usual spelling for the fifth and seventh notes of this motive, even though it means writing a melodic major second as a diminished third.

EXAMPLE 62

EXAMPLE 63: Stravinsky: *Symphony in Three Movements—1st Movement*

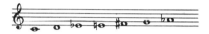

THE TWELVE-TONE TECHNIQUE

One type of basic motive without rhythm that has been developed in this century is deserving of special notice. This is the twelve-tone technique first found in the music of Arnold Schoenberg.

Early applications of the tone row were in music in which tonality was a relatively unimportant means of tonal organization. This music is called *atonal*, a term which is misleading, since it suggests that there is never a key center. In actual practice, key centers are often heard from time to time in atonal music; what is lacking is a clearly defined tonic key and an organization of other keys in relation to it. The practice of using the twelve-tone technique in the writing of atonal music has continued, as if composers are seeking to replace the organizing force of tonality with the relationships of tone rows. Although this practice is common, not all twelve-tone music is atonal and not all atonal music makes use of tone rows.

The basic motive in this music is a group of twelve notes composed of each note of the chromatic scale each of which is used once, called a *tone row*. The tone row is not to be thought of as a scale, for the notes are always used in the same order. In the most strict application of the tone row, some complete form of the row is used to produce every note of the composition. Example 64 shows the tone row from Schoenberg's *Woodwind Quintet*.

EXAMPLE 64

The notes of the row are always used in order, but the row specifies only the order of the notes, not the octave in which each note is to be found. Hence the first two notes may produce a melodic leap of a third, a sixth, or a tenth, and this makes it possible for a composer to use a single row for a long piece without any feeling of repetition. To provide further variety, several traditional devices are applied to the row, resulting in the three further forms of the row seen in Example 65—the inversion (I), the retrograde (R), and the inversion of the retrograde (RI).

EXAMPLE 65

Each of these forms may be transposed to any starting pitch, and these versions may then be identified by giving the form of the row and the starting pitch. Thus Example 64, which is the original (O) form of the row on the starting note E flat may be labeled

O-E flat. The first theme of the Schoenberg *Quintet* (Example 66) illustrates one method of using the row to generate a theme.

EXAMPLE 66:   Schoenberg: *Quintet, Op. 26*

By permission of Mrs. Gertrud Schoenberg.

This row is symmetrical, each half being almost identical, and the biggest division occurring between the two halves of the row. The other basic method of using the row is to distribute the notes vertically among several parts. This technique is shown in Example 67. Here the clarinet part uses the original form of the row on E flat, while the accompaniment uses the inverted form, first on E flat and then on A flat.

EXAMPLE 67

By permission of Mrs. Gertrud Schoenberg.

Example 68 shows the row distributed vertically between all five parts. The forms used are first the original and then the retrograde, so that the movement ends with a chord consisting of the first five notes of the original form of the row. This demonstrates that the row is an important factor in the harmony of a twelve-tone piece as well as in the melodic writing.

Of all the forms of motivic construction discussed in this chapter, the twelve-tone technique is the most intense, and its completely chromatic nature has appealed to many composers in this century. As can be seen from these examples, the tone row structures the composition only to the extent that any basic motive does, and the larger formal organization of the work is still handled like that of more traditional music.

EXAMPLE 68

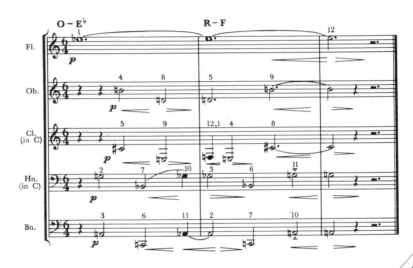

By permission of Mrs. Gertrud Schoenberg.

EXAMPLES FOR ANALYSIS

The works from which the examples for this chapter were taken contain many further examples of the use of motives. The Bach *Fugue in D Major* from the second volume of the *Well-tempered Clavier* and the first movement of the *Fifth Symphony* of Beethoven are examples of an extremely tightly knit construction using motives. The *Symphony in Three Movements* of Stravinsky and the *Second Symphony* of Brahms should be studied to find further examples of the use of their basic motives. Good examples of twelve-tone technique are the *Third* and *Fourth String Quartets* of Schoenberg and the *Violin Concerto* of Alban Berg. The former use the series quite strictly and the latter takes some liberties with the technique, a process that could not be discussed in the text due to lack of space.

IV

Sonata Form

THE NAME *sonata form* must be regarded as a technical term rather than as a descriptive label, since, although it suggests the design of a sonata as a whole, it is actually a formal plan for a single movement of a sonata or a sonata-like work.[1] Sonata form came into being over 200 years ago and has been used constantly from that time to the present. While it is not used as universally today as it once was, it is still popular with composers, and it seems safe to predict that composers will find it useful for some time to come. As is the case of any enduring form, sonata form exists only as a general outline, the details of which are worked out by the composer for a particular

[1] Since it is usually found in the first movement, some authorities prefer the term *first-movement form*, while others, alluding to the fact that first movements are generally fast, prefer the term *sonata-allegro form*. In practice, the form may be used for any movement of a piece and for movements of any tempo, and neither of these labels is therefore very accurate or clear. The term *sonata form* is most commonly used, and is the simplest; therefore it will be used here.

composition. The form is one of those in which a great deal of music grows out of a very small amount of material, thus creating a concise, intense work. A sonata-form movement is one of great scope and complexity, and is an important undertaking for the composer, and one that is approached with some seriousness. The end product may be light and gay or even humorous or witty, but it will still be one that is impressive in its expression. The form will be studied by first considering the general design mentioned above, and then examining some specific works to see the exact details of its application. From such a detailed study, one can learn much more about the form and the great variety that is possible.

THE GENERAL STRUCTURE OF SONATA FORM

A sonata form is divided into three main divisions called the *exposition*, the *development*, and the *recapitulation*. The exposition presents themes, motives, and any other material basic to the movement. The development section subjects materials from the exposition to various metamorphoses and presents them in new relationships. The recapitulation presents again the material of the exposition in a manner similar to its first presentation. In a sense the form is a large, complex ternary form. However, the middle section is never based on new and contrasting material, but rather makes use of material from the first part somehow transformed to give it new meaning. Moreover, unlike some ternary forms, the third section of sonata form is never completely identical with the first section. The greatest difference between sonata form and most ternary forms is that sonata form has a more complex structure for each of its parts, thus creating a movement that is much greater in size and scope than could be achieved with a simple ternary form.

The exposition is dominated by two ideas that are known as the *first theme* and *second theme*.[2] In the simplest possible form these are two melodies that contrast somewhat with one another and are presented as the basic source material for the movement. The first

[2] Many authorities label these *principal theme* and *subordinate theme*. *First* and *second* seems preferable, since both themes are very important to the movement.

theme starts the piece and is always in the tonic key. Since all or fragments of this theme will be treated extensively in the development, and since the return of this theme in its original form will signal the start of the recapitulation, the first theme is usually an emphatic melody that is striking enough to be readily remembered. The second theme which follows is always in some contrasting key. If the piece is in the major, the second theme is most often in the key of the dominant. If the piece is in the minor, the second theme is usually in the key of the dominant minor or the relative major, the choice between the two depending on the mood desired, since one is major and one is minor. Although the second theme is sometimes in some more distantly related key, it is never in the key of the subdominant since, as we have seen before, composers prefer to avoid this key in the early part of a piece. Composers of this century in particular prefer that the key of the second theme be more remote from the tonic than the keys mentioned above.

These two themes and the two key centers constitute the entire minimal requirements for the exposition of a sonata form, but unless the movement is to be a very brief one, there is usually more to be found in an exposition. What is called a *theme* may well be a group of two or more melodies rather than a single one. This is particularly true of a theme-group that is lyric in nature. Here again the standard terminology is rather confusing, since even if a group of four or five melodies is used as a second theme (as Mozart might well do), the term *theme* is used to designate the entire group. The individual melodies are differentiated by referring to them as *second theme, part one*; *second theme, part two*; and so forth. *Part* is an excellent name for these melodies since the term carries with it no prejudice as to size. Sometimes the two theme groups are quite contrasting in nature, one being concise and forceful and the other extensive and lyric. At other times the two themes are much more similar in nature, or nearly identical. The most extreme case of the latter practice is the use of the same melody in both theme groups, as will be shown in the discussion of Haydn's *Symphony No. 104*.

In addition to the two themes, composers generally feel the need for two more elements in an exposition. The first of these is a passage to make a transition between the two themes. There are two major reasons underlying the use of a transitional passage. In the first place, when the first theme is completely presented, it is desirable to lead slowly to the second theme in order to dull the memory of the first, especially if the two themes are greatly contrasting in nature. Secondly, a change of key must take place; if the first theme is to finish in the tonic key and the second theme is to start in its new key, then the modulation must be accomplished in a space that is between the two themes. For these reasons, a passage called a *transition* usually separates the two themes.

Often the second theme is quiet and lyric in nature and so is not suited for use as a climax at the end of the exposition. This function is then supplied by a separate melodic idea that is climactic, which will bring the entire exposition to a very obvious conclusion and so announce the development. This ending melody is called a *closing theme*.[3] In addition to the function of supplying a final climax for the exposition, the closing theme also provides a solid final cadence for the section. Providing this cadence is an important function of the closing theme, and in many early sonata forms the closing theme is not really a separate melodic section, but rather an extended, often stylized, cadence. As in the case of the two theme groups, the closing theme may also be a group of melodies. Some closing themes are material new to the movement, while others make use of ideas presented earlier. Thus many expositions are in reality made up of four sections: the first theme, the transition, the second theme, and the closing theme. Sometimes these are quite separate, but at other times the four sections are fused into a more continuous whole and can be identified only as general areas, not as completely separate sections.

The second big section of a sonata form is the *development*. It is impossible to give a very specific description of this section as a whole, for it is here that composers' imagination is the freest, with the result that no two developments are much alike. A few general observations are possible, but a deep understanding of developments can come only from examining a great many of them in considerable detail. One important feature of the development is that in it tonality becomes more fluid, the piece moves rapidly from key to key, and goes to keys more remote than any of the exposition. It is common also to avoid tonic, so that the sweep of the tonal arch is unbroken. The exposition and recapitulation are static tonally; the development is constantly on the move. All the material of the development is usually related in some way to one of the ideas of the exposition, but each idea is somehow transformed or combined with others.

[3] An alternate name for this section is *codetta,* that is, a little coda used to end a section of a movement.

Therefore the ideas from the exposition cannot be said to be merely repeated, but rather are given new life and new expressiveness. Although the basic function of this section is to develop material that was first heard in the exposition, once in a while one or more new ideas are found in the development section. These are usually also developed, so that the basic nature of the section is not changed. Because examples of new material in a development section can be found, it is necessary to say that the material is *usually* related to the exposition. Sometimes all areas of the exposition will yield material for the development, but often the entire section will grow from two or three ideas or motives, all of which may come from one theme. An extreme example of this sort of thematic or motivic tightness is the Haydn *London Symphony* discussed later in this chapter. A very basic relationship between themes and their development is achieved by the creation in the development of complex passages built entirely upon a motive or motives from one theme of the exposition. It is obvious that composers do not simply write melodies for the exposition and hope that they will contain motives worthy of development. Rather the thematic material for the exposition section of a sonata form is carefully designed to yield expressive and useful motives. This is another reason for the concise pithy first themes that are so common. The development often ends with a passage that creates a feeling of expectancy which culminates in the return of the opening of the movement and consequently in the beginning of the recapitulation. The passage that leads to this return is called the *retransition*. Since the tonic key returns at the moment of the recapitulation, the retransition usually dwells upon the dominant chord of the tonic key and sometimes also upon dominant's dominant.

The *recapitulation* returns the material of the exposition literally or only slightly altered, so that the relationship between this material and its original statement is readily apparent. The entire recapitulation, including the second theme and the closing theme, is in the tonic key. Because the recapitulation is the most static of the three sections in terms of key center, it assures that the movement will end with a very secure sense of the tonic. At least one change must be made in this section, for if the transition from the exposition were to be used unchanged, it would again provide a modulation to the key of the second theme. This section could simply be omitted from the recapitulation, since no modulation is now desired, but this is seldom the case. The transition is reworked to bend it tonally so that when it announces the second theme it does so in the tonic key. From this practice, it is evident that the transition is desired by composers because of the time it occupies in the form, that is, for reasons of design rather than just as a means to move from one key to another. When the tonic key is major, or when the tonic key is minor and the second theme is originally presented in the minor mode, no problem of mode occurs when the second theme is recapitulated. However, if the second theme of a piece whose tonic is minor is presented in the exposition in a major key (probably the relative), then some adjustment is needed in the recapitulation. Sometimes the theme will be returned in the tonic major, in which case the closing theme may well also be major, thus ending the movement in a mood quite different from its start. Sometimes the mode of the second theme is changed to minor, which changes its expression greatly. Mozart is a master of this latter technique; some of his second themes seem to say something completely different when shifted in mode in the recapitulation. A masterful example of this change occurs in the last movement of his *Symphony No. 40 in G Minor*.

Since the exposition and recapitulation may each contain four sections, the development section is usually made up of several distinct sections, and the movement may have an introduction or a coda, it is evident that sonata form is a form of some size and scope.

Example 69 is a diagram of sonata form to help show its structure.

The outline of the form given above is general and in some cases rather vague because of the great variety found in these forms. The subject will be clarified by a detailed look at several movements in sonata form and a consideration of specific details of the form in actual use. A good starting place is the first movement of Beethoven's *Piano Sonata in B Flat, Op. 22*. This is actually as typical a sonata form as Beethoven ever wrote, and one must be careful not to generalize too much from it, for it is difficult to find another sonata form so perfect and satisfying.

Beethoven: *Piano Sonata in B Flat, Op. 22—1st Movement*

Since there is no introduction to this movement, the exposition begins immediately. The first theme, which occupies the first ten and one-half bars, is dominated by the motive in Example 70.

The theme starts hesitatingly and does not really generate any

	Exposition			
Theme	1st theme	Transition	2nd theme	Closing theme
Key	Tonic	Modulating	New key, usually closely related	

melodic feeling until bar 4. A half cadence in bar 11 ends the first theme and brings the start of the transition, which continues to bar 22. The start of the transition uses the motive of the first theme, illustrating a very common practice in sonata form; namely, the use in many passages in the exposition of material from an earlier part

EXAMPLE 70

of the exposition. Thus the process of "development" is found within the exposition as well as in the development itself. This practice reinforces the statement that a sonata form is a large, complex movement based upon a small amount of material that is very highly developed. The transition modulates to the dominant key of F, establishing it by many references to the dominant of F. The second theme, which starts in bar 22, consists of three distinct ideas or parts. Part one starts in bar 22, part two in bar 30, and part three in bar 44. These three parts are not all in the same mood and are not at all equal in melodic value, the outstanding melody of the three being in the second part. This is the melody that is remembered as "the second theme" of this movement. However, the start of the second theme group is located by the solid shift to the dominant key, not by the appearance of an engaging melody, although the term *second theme* suggests that the process of differentiation is largely melodic. The closing theme, which starts in bar 56, consists of two parts. The first of these makes use of an augmented form of the motive from the first theme, shown in Example 71.

Development	Recapitulation			
Themes developed	1st theme	Transistion	2nd theme	Closing theme
Constantly shifting	Entire recapitulation basically tonic			

Part two of the closing theme starts in bar 62 and the dotted rhythm, used in part one of the closing theme and in part two of the second theme, is used to generate a scale and to produce the great

EXAMPLE 71

climax which ends the exposition. While there is no problem in distinguishing between the four sections of the exposition, the ending of the entire exposition is much more conclusive and the break is greater. It is obvious how anxious Beethoven was to make the three big parts of the form clear to his listeners. At the end of bar 68 the pianist is directed to repeat the entire exposition. This was at one time the custom in writing sonata form, but present-day performers are inclined to regard the repeat as optional and frequently omit it. This seems like a good practice in an age in which large amounts of literal repetition are not tolerated very well. Later composers, who did not want the exposition repeated, often drew a double bar at this point which, while it cannot be heard, serves to point out a main juncture in the form to the performer and, incidentally, to the analyst.

Development sections divide readily into parts, since composers are unwilling to produce a long section that does not contain several smaller ones. Sometimes the basis for separating the parts of the development is the progression of key centers, but the usual method of differentiation is to have a series of different treatments of the thematic material. Differences of texture and dynamics are also frequent. It is true that developments generally flow rather continuously, not halting to identify the end of a part. However, the composer is still interested in having the parts stand out clearly, since he has nothing to gain by creating sections and then successfully concealing them from his audience.

The development of this sonata divides into five sections. The first of these, involving the second part of the closing theme, starts in bar 71. It is preceded by a two-bar introduction based on the motive from the first theme which reestablishes the motion after the complete stop that comes at the end of the exposition. The first part of the development starts in F and adds an E flat which suggests a return to the tonic key of B flat. Instead, at the last moment, it slides down to the relative minor and starts the next section with the dominant of this key in bar 75. This second section is based on the first part of the closing theme. At bar 81 begins the third section, which alternates the second part of the closing theme with a sixteenth-note passage using the motive from the first theme. This section passes from G minor to C minor to F minor. The fourth section is by far the longest, and it should be pointed out that not all sections of a development need be the same size. This section (bar 91 through bar 104) uses the main theme motive sequencing upward answered by a descending arpeggio, passing through the keys of F minor, C minor, B flat minor, and A flat. At bar 105 the fifth and last section starts, using the second part of the closing theme in the bass, and presenting successively the dominant of the keys of A flat, F, and B flat. This dominant of B flat starts the retransition, for from this point to the hold there is but one chord, the dominant of the tonic key. As the hold is approached the rhythmic motion diminishes, but the tension and sense of expectation mounts.

As the held chord dies away the listener's attention is completely fixed upon what is to follow, thus dramatically calling his attention to the recapitulation which starts with the pick-up to bar 128. To further help identify the recapitulation, the first theme is returned in a form identical to its first appearance. The transition is now changed so that the second theme will remain in the tonic. Far from considering this section superfluous, Beethoven reworks it to be two bars longer than it was in the exposition. A comparison of these two sections will show where this expansion takes place. The second theme group starts in bar 153 and it and the closing theme are little changed from the exposition, except that they are transposed to the tonic key. The recapitulation ends exactly as the exposition does and in this case the closing theme serves to end the movement.

Sonata forms often have coda sections. This is partly true because so large a movement seems to need a coda to finish it, and also because a climax is necessary. The ending of the exposition is the end of only one section of the movement, and if it is repeated literally no greater conclusion or climax ends the movement as a whole. A coda enables the composer to fashion an even more final-sounding ending for the whole movement.

Note what pains Beethoven takes to make clear in the listener's mind where the main sections of the movement divide. The division between the exposition and development is marked by the very clear and final-sounding ending. The development has no clear conclusion, but gives way to the recapitulation at the moment that the first theme returns, thus making clear the division between the development and the recapitulation. In a typical sonata form the three main parts are very clearly differentiated, and the smaller sections within these parts are also readily seen.

Beethoven: *Symphony No. 7 in A, Op. 92—1st Movement*

The first movement of Beethoven's *Seventh Symphony* is a much more mature and complex work than the piano sonata just considered and provides a large and extremely expressive example of sonata form. In some places this analysis will not go into as much detail, since the reader can do this for himself after studying the last analysis.

The movement has a slow introduction which is not a part of the sonata form. This practice was quite customary in the eighteenth and early nineteenth centuries and is a result of the influence of the slow–fast sections of the French overture. There is no set form to these introductions, and one can only generalize about them. They are in a much slower tempo than the main body of the movement that follows. They start with a very commanding beginning designed to catch the listener's attention, but have no strong conclusion or rounded form, instead dissolving into the movement that they introduce. The introduction of this movement is unusual in that, except for key pattern, it is virtually an abridged sonata form. After this form has been studied in the next chapter, the reader should make a thorough analysis of this introduction.

A very elaborate transition leads to the main body of the movement. Alternating notes between woodwinds and strings generate the dotted eighth – sixteenth – eighth rhythm which is a basic motive of the entire movement. The first theme is presented in bar 67. A second part of the theme occurs in bar 75, and in bar 89 a crescendo culminates in a loud, climactic restatement of the first part of the first theme. Although this movement does not separate the parts by pauses, it is clear that at bar 97 the transition begins, making use of material from the first theme group. Although there is no break in the melodic flow, in bar 119 the key of the dominant (E major) is firmly established and the second theme starts. The second theme is quite climactic, and the two parts of the closing theme (bars 152 and 164) make as great a climax as the piece has had to this point. Since these two high points must not rob each other of effect, they are separated by a contrasting passage. Gradually the climax of the second theme dissipates itself and the piece moves rapidly to a new mood, Beethoven taking the precaution of marking *dolce* in the score. The piece also moves far afield tonally, at bar 136 and following, coming to a cadence and almost complete stop in the key of C major—a very distantly related key. From this point, motion and excitement increase until the start of the closing theme, a climactic point made even more striking by the rise from the very calm passage which preceded it.

This transition-like passage between the second theme and closing theme shows that the concept earlier presented of an exposition dividing into four completely distinct sections is not the only valid description of its structure. In this exposition the clearly identifiable first, second, and closing themes are contained within a fabric that is continuously flowing, thus making hazy the exact boundaries of the theme groups. Expositions, like all parts of a sonata form, differ. The important thing in investigating an exposition is to examine the form for what is really there, not for some preconceived pattern that one believes ought to be there. It is impossible to state too often the basic principle that an analysis must show what the structure really is and what relationships actually give it structure, and not try to prove that the form of the piece fits some preconceived design, sometimes to the point of misinterpreting the piece itself.

After the conventional double bar and repeat sign the development section starts with a repetition of the last bit of the closing theme. In bar 181 the first section of the development starts in the key of C building up a triad in an exact repetition of the start of the exposition. In bar 185 a series of imitative entrances start on a subject related to the first theme. Imitation is a very common device in development sections, since it allows themes to be presented in a new light, and uses a small bit of melodic material to generate a long complex passage. Also, since the texture of expositions tends to be more homophonic, polyphonic passages in the development offer a contrast. This passage leads to the first climax in the development (bar 201) and to the start of the second section. Here again the motive from the first theme is used with some imitation. The key shifts from C to the dominant of A, and so on through a series of keys which should be carefully examined. At bar 220 a sudden drop in dynamics points up the start of the third section. Here is an illustration of how useful composers have found dynamics for making elements of the structure clear to the listener. This section, like the entire development, makes exclusive use of the first theme. This theme, and particularly the rhythmic motive that is found in it, is by far the most striking element in the exposition and the development, recapitulation, and coda are also completely permeated with it.

The material of the third section is used in a new way at bar 236 to start a long build-up which culminates in bar 254 in the biggest climax of the development which, in turn, leads to the retransition. The four-bar passage that preceded the first theme in the exposition returns in bar 274 and the recapitulation begins in bar 278. An interesting reversal of dynamics occurs. The two parts of the first theme, which were presented softly in the exposition, are now presented in the loud, climactic mood that was created by the end of the development. The repetition of the first theme which made the first climax of the exposition (bar 89) is recapitulated as a very quiet, lilting oboe solo (bar 301). Beethoven thus creates a long, continuous climax extending from bar 254 in the development to bar 300. This climax is not interrupted by the start of the recapitulation, yet its continuation does not obscure the recapitulation, since the first theme returns in a manner quite like its first appearance. Other than the necessary reworking of the transition to keep the second theme in the tonic, the recapitulation is very similar to the exposition, even to reaching the key of F major to correspond to the key of C major found midway between the second theme and closing theme in the exposition.

This movement has a very long and elaborate coda which begins in bar 389. Since the composer has provided an easily found end to the exposition, marked by a pause and double bar, the return of this same passage is used to determine exactly where the recapitulation ends and coda begins. This is not always the case; some recapitulations melt into the coda so that it is impossible to point out the exact junction, and all that can be said is that the coda starts in a certain vicinity. This coda makes use of ideas from the first theme group in a way that can only be said to be developmental. Beethoven concluded many of his sonata forms with an elaborate coda such as this one. The sonata form of this movement can be said to have four equal parts—exposition, development, recapitulation, and coda. Composers following Beethoven, such as Schumann and Brahms, were influenced to also write long, elaborate, developmental codas. Like the development, the coda may be divided into sections according to the treatment of the material. But since it is to end the movement, the coda remains in or near the tonic key. This means that the second half of the movement is nearly all tonic, an interesting design of tonal arch. This coda begins with a humorous echo of the end of the closing theme in bar 389. The first section is very subdued and is based on the opening of the first theme. There follows in bar 401 a second section which begins another long crescendo passage. Over a two-bar ostinato in the bass instruments, the violins play a repeated figure which becomes more rhythmically agitated on every repetition until it bursts into a great climax at bar 423 that continues to the end of the movement. At bar 442 the winds, principally the horns, make the greatest climax of the movement, using the opening of the first theme. The sonata form is thus completely rounded, the same bar of melody coming at the beginning and at the very end. It is as if Beethoven, having made a coda which is like a second development section, felt obliged to once again refer to, or recapitulate, the first theme. This practice is common in a movement with a long coda.

A very important feature of the structure of this movement is the feeling of motion created by a series of very carefully controlled climaxes. It is easy to give such attention to the parts of the structure and to other items that tend to make the piece become a series of bits, that the over-all organization of the piece is lost. Before leaving this movement, let us consider the effect of the climaxes to see how Beethoven uses their ebb and flow to maintain a constant state of flux. The movement's first climax comes in bar 15 in the introduction. This climax is maintained for several bars and then a calmer theme enters. In bar 34 the climax from bar 15 is restated. Since they are identical, these two climaxes are equal. As noted before, the first theme of the exposition starts calmly and builds up to a climax at bar 89. This is probably no louder than the two in the introduction, but the faster tempo and greater rhythmic motion make for a greater degree of excitement. Several further climaxes follow, leading to the very quiet, almost static spot that precedes the closing theme. The closing theme opens with the greatest climax in the movement so far, but even it begins at a lower level than the point finally reached in bar 164 (closing theme, part two). The high points of the development have been treated in the previous discussion of that section. Especially noteworthy is the dramatic drop to a calm passage that occurs in bar 220. The long climax at the end of the development, retransition, and first part of the recapitulation has already been discussed. This is as great a climax as has yet occurred, partly because its great length generates so much excitement. The succeeding high points of the recapitulation, including the closing theme, duplicate the corresponding spots in the exposition. This makes clear how much Beethoven needed a coda with an even greater climax to sum up the whole movement. Notice how successfully he achieves this by starting with a long, calm passage marked *sempre pp* followed by a long build-up of tension created by the repetitious ostinato in the bass. At last, in bar 423, comes the movement's greatest climax created by loudness, forcefulness of scoring, and rhythmic excitement. But even this did not satisfy Beethoven, who felt obliged to create one final, overpowering climax at bar 442. This, the movement's highest point, comes just seven measures from the end. It is interesting to speculate whether Beethoven, after he worked out the design for this series of climaxes, wrote each of them so as to be sure that they came in ascending order of excitement, or whether he wrote the movement more nearly in order, being confident each time he wrote a climax that, no matter how exciting it was, he had the skill to exceed it when there was need to. If the latter was the case, then the high point of the movement was created in a moment of supreme inspiration.

Beethoven: *Symphony No. 7 in A, Op. 92—Finale*

Although there is no need to treat this movement in great detail, there are several points in it that are worth noting. The first theme consists of three parts, each of which is repeated, the last repeat being written out so that the scoring can be changed. This theme is followed by a transition which leads to the second theme at bar 63. This second theme is in an unusual key—C sharp minor, the key of the mediant. The rest of the exposition remains in this key, the closing theme in bar 104 being also in C sharp minor. A striking feature of the development is the presentation, at bar 147, of the first two parts of the first theme, complete with repeats, in the key of C major.

This key is especially effective after the long use of C sharp minor in the exposition. A long climax follows these two repeated strains, but at the moment when a final build-up to an even greater climax is expected, the dynamic level falls and a very gentle passage proceeds the recapitulation. Since the first two parts of the first theme were used literally in the development, the first theme group in the recapitulation (bar 221 forward) contains only the first and third parts of the theme, again with each part repeated. The second theme is recapitulated in the tonic key of A, but here Beethoven has a problem of mode. He solves this by sometimes using A minor, as in bar 275, and sometimes changing the mode to A major, as in bar 286. This alternation of mode continues through the closing theme which appears in bar 320. The long coda is based on the first theme, part three of that theme being used in its entirety (including the usual repeat) starting in bar 406. The plan of climaxes of this movement will be discussed in Chapter VII as a part of the discussion of the form of this whole symphony.

FURTHER GENERAL DESCRIPTION OF THE FORM

Now that two developments have been analyzed, some further observations about the development section are possible. While this section usually draws its material from the exposition, composers are no more consistent about this than about any other detail. In a few cases, new material is introduced in this section, which may be then subjected to development, or simply stated, perhaps repeated, and then left. Mozart was particularly fond of this technique, as would be expected in one of his great melodic gift.

An illuminating example of new material in the development is found in the *Eroica Symphony* of Beethoven. During the development (bar 284) a new theme is introduced, a theme as melodically important as the main themes of the movement. After its presentation, this theme is developed somewhat, along with material from the exposition. This new theme is not found at all in the recapitulation, but in the coda it is returned (bar 581). Thus material presented first in the exposition is returned in the recapitulation, and material presented first in the development is returned in the coda, a clear demonstration of the linking of the development and coda in Beethoven's mind, and a further suggestion that, to Beethoven, the sonata form had four equal parts. This idea is further borne out by the fact that these parts are nearly the same in length. This device of thematic relationship between the development and coda is not one that Beethoven chose to use again, and although Mendelssohn introduced new themes in developments in his *Italian Symphony* and in the *Hebrides Overture*, he did not recapitulate them in the coda.

Large sections of developments are often constructed of chains or sequences of melodic material or of key centers. The key may shift up or down in a series of seconds or thirds, or move in either direction in the circle of fifths. The mode may stay the same during the tonal motion, or it may alternate major and minor or make some other such pattern. All of these techniques create the feeling of motion from place to place typical of the development section. In the course of this motion a pattern may well pass through the tonic key. It cannot therefore be said that the tonic key is never found in the development, but rather that it is not an important key. In orchestral music written before the development of the valved brass instruments and the pedal timpani, a large climax depended upon being close enough to the tonic key to allow the brass and percussion to be used fully. This limitation sometimes has an effect on the key patterns of early orchestral sonata forms. In a similar way any sonata form reflects the nature of the medium for which it is written.

Early composers of sonata forms depended a great deal on the shift from the tonic to a new key to identify the second theme. Later composers, writing in a more chromatic era when shifts of key came more often and were harder to follow, were forced to seek other means to separate the two theme groups. Also, since early sonata forms were shorter pieces, the material was necessarily more nearly of the same mood.

Haydn was very fond of a device that, although he used it extensively and although he had great influence on those that followed him, was never used much by later composers. His practice was to use as the second theme the melody of the first theme transposed to the new key. Although sometimes the melody was changed very slightly to show that it was in a new theme group, it was usually quite unchanged, and often set with exactly the same scoring to emphasize the similarity. Mozart, too, sometimes used this technique, although he usually made a small change in the melody when it was serving as a second theme. The need of later composers to make greater contrasts of mood between themes led to the abandonment of this practice. At the same time, one can see how much

Haydn depended upon key rather than contrast of melody to distinguish between his themes.

A good illustration of this technique is the first movement of Haydn's *Symphony No. 104 in D*, the London Symphony. In bar 49 the melody of the first theme is quoted by the violins exactly as they first presented it, except that it is now in the key of the dominant. Since this theme follows a normal transition section, the key is the one expected, and there is no other melody at this point, it must be considered the second theme. In the recapitulation both "themes" are returned, even though one appearance would suffice to present this melody in the tonic. The first theme occurs at bar 177 and the second theme at bar 231, the second theme being altered slightly with some imitation for the sake of variety. This whole movement is well worth studying, as it contains one of Haydn's greatest development sections. The entire section is based on a motive derived from the third and fourth bars of the first and only theme. The movement is entirely monothematic, and one wonders why this practice has not been used more often.

The principles that have been observed in the previous examples would be equally applicable to any other movement that is in sonata form, or to an overture or other one-movement piece that uses the form. Slow movements move so slowly that a long time is spent in each section, and for this reason composers sometimes limit the less essential sections (transition or closing theme) to a bare minimum of time. Very fast movements present material rapidly, and each section needs to be quite extensive if the movement is not to be very short.

Bruckner, Mahler, and other composers of the late nineteenth century wrote gigantic sonata forms, some lasting as long as 20 minutes. In general outline these movements exhibit the basic elements of the form, but there is much elaboration of detail to produce so large a structure. The material of these movements presents a great variety of moods, suggesting that if a single movement is to last as long as an entire symphony of Haydn, it must contain as much variety of theme and mood as one of his symphonies. Mahler's music furnishes very good examples of extended sonata movements. Successful analysis of this music depends upon starting with a study of the main outline of the movement, even though the large size makes it much easier to see the details than the main structure.

The composer of the twentieth century is more likely to write a much smaller sonata form, and one that reflects the technical changes of this century. A single key center lasts longer in a modern piece, which means that contemporary development sections do not shift key as rapidly as those by earlier composers. Key center is still an important element of formal design, but composers do not rely on it as the sole means of differentiating themes or sections as the composers of the Classic Era occasionally did. Separation of material is also provided by changes of mood and tempo. Those composers who do not use key center as a means of formal design (the so-called *Atonalists*) use all the other elements of the form to make highly successful sonata movements. The contemporary composer is very fond of an arch form in which the beginning and end are identical, and the intervening material first moves away from and then returns to the material of the opening. To achieve this effect the order of the material is inverted, so that the recapitulation starts with the closing theme, progresses to the second theme, and ends with the first theme. The composer often feels that, since the beginning and end are alike, no coda is possible. The coda section, which grew in size throughout most of the last century, is today either rather small or even nonexistent. When the order of themes is inverted in the recapitulation, the section may not be in the tonic key; often only the first theme, which closes the recapitulation, is in the tonic, thus prolonging the span of the tonal arch. However, if all the themes are not recapitulated in the tonic, then the fact that a recapitulation is in progress must be conveyed by the literalness of the return. Perhaps the success of this technique depends in part on the fact that listeners have had over two centuries of experience with sonata form. Such an inverted recapitulation is described in the next analysis.

Stravinsky: *Octet—1st Movement*

The sonata form of this movement is preceded by a slow introduction in a rather free form. Late in the introduction the material of the opening returns. At number 6 the first theme is presented in the tonic key, E flat, and at 7 and 8 the theme is repeated imitatively. At 9 the imitation occurs once more with the time interval between the two parts in the trumpets and woodwinds reduced to an eighth note. The theme is therefore played by the flute and clarinet in syncopated quarter notes, which, in turn, foreshadow the second theme. From number 8 on the key has been shifting, and at 10 the second theme enters in the key of D. This tonal relationship of a second between themes is very common in modern music, as are other remote relationships such as the tritone. At 11, the second trumpet introduces a second part to the second theme, and at 12 the first part of the second theme is again presented, now in the key of A flat.

Since at 13 the second theme has ended, the development must start here. However, there are no separate sections as such, and it is impossible to say that at one certain spot a particular section begins. Also, there is no separate transition and no closing theme, and the key center is constantly moving, so that the whole movement is in a constant state of flux. The development is mostly concerned with developing the figure of two sixteenth notes and an eighth note that was first presented by the bassoons at number 9. Several little passages occur more than once in the development, such as the spot 5 bars after 13 which comes again at 17, and the spot at 14 which returns at 15. None of the material in the development seems new, but rather is related by motive and spirit to the exposition.

At the end of the fourth bar after 17 the second trumpet, the original instrument, sneaks in the second part of the second theme, and this starts the recapitulation. At 18 the first part of the second theme returns in the key of E. Although in the exposition the second theme was first presented a half-step below tonic, here it is a half-step above, showing Stravinsky's remarkable interest in symmetry. At 19 the bassoon and second trumpet introduce an imitative passage on a new theme which is nevertheless closely related to all that has come before. This passage delays the return of the first theme, thus building up a tension that focuses the listener's attention on the return of this theme at number 21. Here at last the tonic key returns, and with the return of this theme and key the movement has fulfilled itself, and soon comes to a close after stating the first theme imitatively at 23. Note how completely this form fits the description of the arch form, starting and ending with the first theme tonic, moving slowly away from it and then retracing its steps to end.

Not all contemporary sonata forms invert the recapitulation; some use the traditional order and others use other variant orders. Nevertheless, such movements still fit the general description of the form given earlier, and although the form has changed in this century it has not lost its identity. The flexibility of the sonata form is the reason that composers are still able to write original and individual works in a form that is so old and so much used.

Extensive as this chapter has been, it constitutes but an introduction to the subject of sonata form. This form and that of the fugue are two of the most complex of musical structures, and each is deserving of much more extensive study. The next step in becoming better acquainted with sonata form is the detailed study of a large number of these forms written in different eras by various composers for a variety of performing media. Although each will conform in essence to the general outline as presented, each will offer a rich variety of detail that will further illuminate the nature of this form.

EXAMPLES FOR ANALYSIS

The past 200 years have produced so many examples of sonata form that any list of examples for study can hardly be regarded as more than a random sample. Although this form is usually used for first movements, slow movements and finales which use it should also be studied so that the form can be seen in many different kinds of movements.

Beethoven: *Piano Sonata No. 15, Op. 28—1st Movement*

Beethoven: *Piano Sonata No. 11, Op. 22—2nd Movement*

Beethoven: *Piano Sonata No. 14, Op. 27, No. 2* (Moonlight) *— Finale*

Mozart: *Symphony No. 38 in D, K. 504* (Prague)—All three movements of this symphony are in sonata form and offer an excellent example of the variety possible in movements using the same form.

Examples of this form from the Romantic Era should also be examined. A good example of the use of the form to construct a large movement is furnished by the first movement of the *Second Symphony* (Resurrection) of Mahler. The following movements from the twentieth century are recommended as being very clear.

Bartók: *Concerto for Orchestra*—1st and last movements

Bartók: Fifth String Quartet—*1st Movement*

Stravinsky: *Symphony in C—1st Movement*

Hindemith: *Symphony Mathis der Maler—1st Movement.* In this movement the introduction is incorporated into the recapitulation.

Prokofiev: *Third Piano Concerto—1st Movement*

Prokofiev: *Classical Symphony*—First and last movements

V

Variants of
Sonata Form

THE WIDE INFLUENCE that sonata form has exerted on instrumental music since early in the Classic Era is evident in many areas of the literature. Not only are there a great many movements in this form, but it has also influenced the design of older forms. This chapter presents three common variants of sonata form, each of which can be clarified by a discussion of its relationship to that form.

ABRIDGED SONATA FORM

Composers sometimes wish to use the general procedures of the exposition of sonata form to present the material of a composition and a recapitulation section to return each of the themes of the exposition, but do not wish a development section. This may be because the nature of the movement is essentially lyric and the fragmentation involved in development would interrupt the flow of melody, or because the movement is very slow and an extensive development section would be intolerably long, or for some other compelling reason. This desire leads to a simple abridgement of sonata form in which a normal exposition is followed directly by a normal recapitulation, and the development section is completely omitted from the work. Since this is an incomplete version of a familiar form, no new term is needed to identify it, and it is called *abridged sonata form*.[1] The transition from the end of the exposition to the recapitulation is accomplished either by having the end of the closing theme modulate back to the tonic key, or by ending the closing theme in its key and adding a short bridge passage to prepare for the recapitulation. The first theme group in the recapitulation may be extended and altered, sometimes even dipping into the other mode. This extension may be almost developmental in nature, showing that although the development section is rejected for this form, the urge to have some developing of the thematic material is strong. Although no new analysis problem is encountered in this form, it is desirable to look at two examples. The overture by Mozart discussed first is a typical example of the form and serves also to show certain techniques of exposition and recapitulation that are typical of Mozart. The example by Brahms that follows is not analyzed thoroughly, but is outlined in sufficient detail to enable the reader to make a thorough analysis.

Mozart: *Overture to the Marriage of Figaro*

The first part of the first theme, which opens this overture, is followed directly by part two in bar 8. The entire first theme is then repeated, a woodwind obbligato being added to the first part. Bar 35 is clearly the start of the transition, but no modulation occurs, the transition ending instead with a half cadence in the tonic key (D major). This dominant chord leads smoothly to the second theme which starts at once in the dominant key. There is no better example of Mozart's great melodic gift and its influence on his formal procedures than the series of melodic ideas contained in this theme group. Part one occurs in bar 59, part two in bar 75, part three in bar 85, and part four in bar 108. As in the Beethoven *Piano Sonata in B Flat, Op. 22*, the melody of the last part is the

[1] Some authorities call this form *sonatina form*. Since a number of composers have called short, multi-movement, sonata-like works by this name, and since many of these works contain complete sonata forms, *sonatina form* seems misleading.

most engaging, and the one that is most likely to be remembered as "the second theme." The closing theme starts in bar 123. Late in this theme Mozart adds a G natural to the tonic chord of the key of A, thus creating the dominant seventh chord of D to lead to the recapitulation, which occurs in bar 139 following a short passage in the violins that serves as a link back to the first theme. In bar 156 the first part of the first theme is extended and altered somewhat in a way that suggests the start of a development. This is the practice mentioned earlier of suggesting a development in the early part of the recapitulation. The early part of the transition is suppressed, but the end of it is returned literally, bars 164-171 being an exact repetition of bars 51-58 in the exposition. Since the A major triad at the end of this passage is both the tonic chord of the key of A and the dominant chord of the key of D, the second theme can follow equally well in either key, thus making it unnecessary to change the transition in any way in the recapitulation. The composers of the Classic Era were very fond of this device, sometimes using the entire transition unchanged in the recapitulation, and sometimes using just the latter part of it. The parts of the second theme follow in order, part one coming at bar 172, part two at bar 188, part three at bar 198, and part four at bar 221. The closing theme is altered to lead to a climax at bar 252 which makes extensive use of the material first presented in the exposition in bar 45, in that part of the transition that was previously omitted. This passage is the coda to the work, a coda that is created by rearranging the material in the recapitulation, withholding an earlier climatic passage to use it at the end as a coda. This also is a favorite device of the classical composer, who seeks to return all the material of the exposition only once in the recapitulation, but rearranges it to make the biggest climax come at the end of the recapitulation and hence at the end of the work.

Brahms: *Symphony No. 1 in C Minor—Finale*

This movement is one of the largest examples of this form to be found, and serves to illustrate the fact that a simple form does not always result in a short, simple movement. The main body of the movement is preceded by an extensive introduction. All of the ideas in this introduction are used again later in the movement, so that no idea is presented once and then forgotten.

The first theme, which starts the main body of the movement, comes at the *Allegro* in bar 62. The beginning of this theme uses an idea found in the first bar of the introduction. The second theme, which begins in bar 118, is introduced by an idea in bar 114 first found in bar 30 of the introduction. The closing theme (bar 148) is based on the woodwind melody in bar 22 of the introduction and is extended to lead to the recapitulation at bar 186. Following this there is an extremely long and complex extension of the first theme group. Some of this is the developmental passages that is so often found at this place in this form, but there is also another reference to the introduction when, in bar 208, material from bar 5 is presented. The rest of the recapitulation progresses as expected, and at bar 367 an extensive coda begins, largely using material from the exposition, as was Beethoven's practice. However, in bar 407 the chorale-like melody first found in bar 47 of the introduction is returned and used to make a very dramatic climax. Brahms has now restated all the important ideas of the introduction, thus adding a dimension to the normal design of an abridged sonata form.

SONATA-RONDO FORM

Soon after the development of sonata form, elements of its design began to affect the structure of the rondo, and a new form was produced which is really a hybrid of these two. For this reason the form is termed *sonata-rondo form*, instead of some new name. Throughout the Classic and Romantic Eras sonata-rondo largely replaced the rondo form previously studied. When a composer called a movement a *rondo,* he probably had written a sonata-rondo. In this century, this form in turn has given way to the older type of rondo, and although the sonata-rondo was once used extensively, it is no longer of much interest to composers. Its basic structure is this: the work starts with the rondo theme [2] as usual,

[2] As can be seen, the terminology used for the various parts of this form is derived partly from the terminology of sonata form and partly from that of rondo. Other derivations of terms are obviously possible, so that one could use *first theme* for *rondo theme, first episode* for *second theme,* and call the middle episode *second episode.* The author prefers the terms used above since they label the various sections with the term from the parent forms which seems most descriptive. If the form were expressed in letter names it would be: A B A C A B A, where A is always in the tonic key, the first B is not tonic and the second B is.

but in place of the first episode there is what seems to be the second theme of a sonata form in one of the usual second theme keys. This is followed by the return of the rondo theme in the tonic key. There follows a middle episode which consists of new material and is in some previously unused key, often the subdominant. Following this the rondo theme returns in the tonic key followed by the second theme, which is now also in the tonic key, followed by one last appearance of the rondo theme.

This sounds complicated, but a consideration of the rondo elements and the sonata-form elements in the form may simplify it. Like any other rondo, this form has at least three appearances of the rondo theme; in the typical case outlined above, four. Also, the rondo theme's appearances are separated by episode-like passages which present contrasting material rather than developing material from the rondo theme. However, unlike the simple rondo form, the first episode is recapitulated later in the tonic key, a treatment similar to the second theme of sonata form. Like a sonata, the second theme is usually preceded by a transition section and may be followed by a closing theme; indeed, at the end of the presentation of the rondo theme, transition, and second theme, the form may well be identical to a sonata form. What comes next immediately establishes the identity of the form since a sonata form would not, at this point, return the entire first theme in the tonic key. This is the first spot to examine when trying to distinguish a sonata-rondo form from a sonata form. As one would expect in a hybrid form, composers sometimes construct these forms to be more like one of the two parent forms than the other. The two elements necessary for sonata-rondo form are the return of the rondo theme in the tonic key between the second theme and middle episode, and a second theme group which is first presented in a contrasting key and later recapitulated in the tonic. The form thus contains a vital element from each of the two parent forms. Another variant of this form is the use of a developmental section to replace all or part of the middle episode, a device that tends more in the direction of sonata form. Often the composer is dissatisfied with the effect of so many literal appearances of the rondo theme, and so replaces the last of these with a coda based on it, thus retaining a suggestion of it. A very typical example of sonata-rondo is the last movement of the Beethoven *Piano Sonata, Op. 22,* that was examined earlier for the sonata form of the first movement.

Beethoven: *Piano Sonata in B Flat, Op. 22—Rondo*

The rondo theme, which opens the movement, is repeated in bar 9 in a fuller setting. The rondo theme ends in bar 18, and a short transition leads to the second theme in the dominant key (bar 22). This transition is based on a new idea that is to be used repeatedly in the movement. At bar 32 the second theme gives way to a closing theme such as is commonly found in a sonata form. Until an E flat in the bass in bar 37 starts a return to the tonic key of B flat, the movement gives no indication of not being a sonata form. However, instead of the development which would follow in sonata form, an elaborate bridge leads to a return of the rondo theme in the tonic key in bar 50. Sonata-rondos never call for the performer to repeat the exposition as sonata forms so often do. Also, instead of breaking completely at the end of the exposition as is common in sonata form, a sonata-rondo usually flows continuously from second theme through closing theme (if any) and into a bridge back to the rondo theme. Note in this example how much expectancy is created before the rondo theme returns.

Except for some melodic elaboration, the rondo theme is presented exactly as before, ending in bar 67. A short bridge based on material from the transition leads to the middle episode, which is a ternary form and lasts from bar 72 to bar 103. It introduces a new theme at the beginning, but in its middle section develops the motive from the transition. After another bridge the rondo theme returns in bar 112. Following the transition (bar 129) the second theme is recapitulated in the tonic key in bar 135. The closing theme follows and again leads to a bridge that, in turn, leads to a false return of the rondo theme in the subdominant key in bar 153. This breaks off into an imitative passage which leads to the final return of the rondo theme in bar 165. This time the melody is the subject of considerable figuration, but it is exactly the same length as it was on its other three appearances. A coda starts in bar 182, once again making use of the idea first found in the transition. After one final reference to the opening of the rondo theme, the movement ends.

This is a typical sonata-rondo. It is a form that is quite logical for eras that were dominated by sonata form, but one feels that in the composer's mind the form is always a rondo with sonata-form overtones. Two characteristics of rondo are found in this movement and in most sonata-rondos: the continuous flow from part to part, and the light, gay character of the themes and hence of the movement. This is the greatest heritage of this form from the simple rondo of earlier times. As is true of the movement just studied, composers generally title such a movement *Rondo*, as if to inform the player and listener from the start of the sort of movement to follow. Examination of a number of rondos, whether sonata-rondos or simple rondos, will bear this out.

Beethoven: *Symphony No. 7 in A Major—2nd Movement*

After even a brief study of the form of this movement, it must be concluded that the details of its structure are not completely like any form previously presented. In the whole literature there is not another movement quite like this, even in Beethoven's own music.[3] For this reason, the mere attaching of the label of one of the common forms to this movement will contribute little to its understanding. At the same time, since Beethoven did not write the movement in a vacuum, it must reflect the formal practices common to his style. Beethoven used the sonata-rondo form as a point of departure, altering it greatly to suit his purpose. It is of little consequence to argue whether the movement "is" a sonata-rondo or not, but an analysis that considers the main outline and terminology of this form will help shed light on the movement's structure.

A tonic chord in the winds starts the movement. The rondo theme, which is found in bar 3 in the violas, is 24 measures long, the last eight bars of the theme being a repeat of the second eight bars played at a softer dynamic level. This eight-bar echo is usually present in the theme. In bar 27 there occurs a variation of the theme, the second violins playing it, while the violas and cellos play a countermelody which is much more expressive than the theme itself. At bar 51 the first violins enter with the theme, the countermelody passes to the second violins, and the violas and cellos play a second countermelody. This is a second variation, and throughout it a long crescendo leads to a third variation at bar 75. This variation is a climax, with the theme forcefully stated by the winds, the first countermelody taken very high by the first violins, and the second countermelody played by the second violins. The last eight bars of the theme make an extreme diminuendo, and at bar 100 the rondo theme ends very quietly. All that has occurred to this

[3] The movement is studied here partly to show how an offshoot of a common form can be treated and partly to include in the book analyses of all four movements of this symphony.

point has been the first section or presentation of the rondo theme. This has occupied a great deal of space, since not only is the theme itself long, but it is followed by three variations. The series of entrances of the theme and the typically used countersubjects give a hint of the form of a fugue, so that actually this section, which is the first section of a rondo, has also aspects of two other forms.[4]

The tonality immediately changes to the tonic major, and the bassoon and clarinet present the second theme. This is followed in bar 117 by part two of the second theme. However, A major is not a sufficient contrast to A minor to serve as a satisfactory key for the second theme, so in bar 135 the key shifts to C, the relative major—a key commonly used for second themes. This theme breaks off almost at once, and at bar 150 we find the second appearance of the rondo theme accompanied by the first countermelody in the woodwinds. In a sense this is also the fourth variation of the rondo theme, thus continuing the suggestion that more than one form is involved in this movement.

After a complete presentation of the rondo theme, the woodwinds extend the countermelody to lead to a developmental passage in bar 183. While most sonata-rondos have a middle episode here, some, including this one, have a development instead. The development consists of the imitative use of a motive from the rondo theme. The whole section is an unbroken string of sixteenth notes, and at the cresendo in bar 210 these generate increasing excitement. Just as the crescendo reaches its climax, the sixteenth notes in the strings pass to the woodwinds and the rondo theme appears for the third time in the strings. Since one would expect the strings to continue the sixteenth notes and the winds to enter with the rondo theme, Beethoven's dramatic switch of parts heightens the excitement of the recapitulation. The rondo theme is not complete here, only the first eight measures being used. (This movement has extremely unusual proportions; the first appearance of the rondo theme occupies some 98 measures, the second appearance 24 measures, and the third 8 measures.) This is followed immediately by the second theme, which returns exactly as it was first presented, but is shortened to omit the last section which modulated to the relative major. This is one of the most unusual and imaginative techniques in the movement; the second theme is first presented

[4] Theme and Variations and Fugue, both of which will be discussed in later chapters. After these have been studied, the first section of this movement should be restudied.

in the tonic major with a modulation late in its course to take it to the relative major. It is then kept in the tonic in the recapitulaion by omitting the last part so that only the first section remains. The movement ends with a brief coda, but bars 255-270 also contain the first sixteen bars of the rondo theme. At the very end of the movement the woodwinds play the same chord that started the movement and so the cycle is complete.

Before leaving this form, mention should be made of Mozart's solution to the problem of the large number of literal repetitions in this form. Mozart wrote sonata-rondos that are normal in every respect except that the third appearance of the rondo theme is suppressed. This makes the form rondo theme – second theme – rondo theme – middle episode – second theme – rondo theme. The key centers of the two second-theme appearances are normal, so that the return of the second theme in the tonic successfully creates the feeling of recapitulation. Notice that the second theme – rondo theme recapitulation is the inverted order of recapitulation found in some contemporary sonata forms. Composers after Mozart made no great use of this variant of sonata-rondo, although there are examples by both Beethoven and Brahms, among others. Instead of suppressing the third appearance of the rondo theme, later composers preferred to make the fourth appearance of the rondo theme into a coda, thus reducing the number of repetitions of the rondo theme. Some examples of Mozart's variant are included in the examples at the end of the chapter.

DOUBLE EXPOSITION FORM IN THE CONCERTO

Because of its medium, the concerto poses special problems of balance and organization for the composer. Such unlike elements as a soloist and an entire symphony orchestra must be so successfully joined that the presence of each is justified. If the soloist predominates too much of the time, there seems no need to use an entire orchestra for the accompaniment, while if the orchestra is too prominent, the work becomes a symphony with an obbligato part for the soloist. Thus to achieve a balance the composer must give important duties to each. The techniques used by composers of the Baroque Era to achieve this balance will be discussed in Chapter VIII. The composers of the Classic and Romantic Eras often made use of a modification of sonata form in the first movement of a concerto based on the practice of repeating the exposition discussed in the last chapter. In a concerto the repeated material is written out. The orchestra plays the entire first exposition by itself, and the soloist dominates the second exposition.

While equality is sought by featuring half of the medium in each exposition, an imbalance in the favor of the orchestra results, because all material is first presented by the orchestra. For this reason, certain other practices are common. Many times the second theme and closing theme are kept in the tonic key in the first exposition, leaving the presentation of any new key, and the interest that this brings, to the solo part in the second exposition. In this case, the second theme must be identified by some means other than by the shift to a new key. Sometimes one or more theme groups are incomplete in the first exposition, and new thematic material is left for the soloist to present in the second exposition. Nearly always the second exposition is more extensive than the first, since it is also augmented by passages commonly found in concertos that demonstrate the technical prowess of the soloist. The first exposition usually ends with a closing theme to indicate that this exposition is ending and the soloist is about to enter. The second exposition needs no such definite ending and often flows smoothly into the development, frequently in a way that makes it impossible to identify the exact moment that the development begins.

Since neither the development nor recapitulation are repeated, a balance between the orchestra and soloist is provided by having some passages feature each member. The recapitulation is made in part of passages from the first exposition and in part of passages from the second exposition, alternated in an extremely ingenious fashion. After the recapitulation has concluded, and sometimes after a coda has begun, the orchestra grows to a climax ending on a long, loud, held tonic six-four chord. This is followed by a free passage of complex technical display, played by the soloist alone, called a *cadenza*. This ends with a long trilled note and a suggestion of the dominant chord, after which the orchestra re-enters on a loud tonic chord and, without the soloist, rapidly brings the movement to an end. The cadenza is an elaboration of the dominant seventh chord of a final strong cadence: tonic six-four—dominant seventh—tonic. Thus the last chord of the cadenza must be a dominant. Early in the history of this form the cadenza was improvised by the soloist, and the convention of ending the cadenza with a long trill signaled the orchestra that they should re-enter. Later, as the era of improvisation died out, it became the custom of the composer to write out the cadenza, but the practice of ending with a trill remained. Cadenzas may be inserted by the composer in other places in the movement, such as between the devlopment and the recapitulation. Cadenzas may also be found in other movements in the concerto, but the most common location is after the recapitulation in the first movement. By the Romantic Era, composers began to abandon the practice of writing double exposition first movements, instead achieving balance by alternating groups in the single exposition, and in this century the form has fallen into complete disuse.

Double Exposition form in the Concerto

Mozart: *Piano Concerto in B Flat, K. 595—1st Movement*

No composer exceeds Mozart in the ability to achieve an absolute balance between soloist and orchestra, and therefore there is no better place to start a study of the double exposition form than with one of his concertos. These have served as models for the achievement of this balance, and have had great influence on all composers since his time.

The movement starts with the orchestra's exposition, the first violins playing part one of the first theme with part two following in bar 13. Since the second theme is tonic, there is no need of a transition, and the second theme group starts in bar 16. There are a number of parts to the second theme group and naming them poses a problem. This is because two parts of this theme group are not presented in this exposition, but are reserved for the soloist's exposition. Furthermore, while the theme in bar 16 starts this group in the first exposition, it is part three in the second exposition. The most successful solution to this problem is to first analyze the second theme group in the second exposition, labeling each part, and then apply these labels to those parts that are found in the first exposition. This technique also insures an accurate analysis of the second theme group, since in the first exposition the lack of any key but tonic may obscure the identity of all parts of the second theme. In accordance with this practice, bar 16 is called part three of the second theme, and bar 29 is part four.

The closing theme [5] starts in bar 47 and consists of three parts found in bars 47, 55, and 69. The last of these brings the first exposition to a complete close.

The soloist immediately starts the second exposition, playing the first part of the first theme. The orchestra presents part two of the first theme in bar 85, which is greatly extended to give the soloist a chance to play it as well. In bar 99 a half cadence in the key of B flat leads immediately to the second theme in the key of the dominant minor. Now, for the first time, the soloist introduces the first part of the second theme (bar 100), presenting at the same time the first change of key in the movement. This gives an important function to the piano and helps compensate for the large amount of new material that the orchestra presented in the first exposition. The mode shifts to F major with part two of the second theme in bar 115, and part three follows in bar 123. Part four occurs first in the violins in bar 136 and is repeated by the piano, thus giving the orchestra one chance to be featured in the second theme group. An entirely new closing theme group is provided in bar 146, one that doesn't come to a complete close, but rather breaks off in bar 180 and leads directly into the development.

The development starts with the piano playing the first theme in the key of B minor, a key distantly related to the tonic and in opposite mode. This is followed by an answering figure from the first theme in the orchestra, followed in bar 190 by part one of the first theme in C major in the piano. Again the answering figure follows, first in the strings, then in the woodwinds, and then in the piano. Throughout the development there is a constant interplay between the soloist and the orchestra, so that each contributes something to the flow of this section and to the process of development. The remainder of the development is devoted to a series of entrances of these same two melodic ideas from the first theme until the retransition begins, using the second part of the first theme. Although the second theme and closing theme have a great number of parts, these are not used at all in the development, for

[5] From the beginning of the second theme group to the end of the exposition there occur a series of melodies which sound progressively more and more like closing-theme material. In such a case the selection of one of these melodies as the first part of the closing theme is clearly arbitrary, and only to an extent meaningful. It is not necessary that the composer designate one spot as the junction between these two parts of a form, and Mozart has not made a clear distinction here.

if a development is to be as tightly knit as this one, it must limit itself to a small amount of thematic material. The entire development section is characterized by a restless series of modulations. A listing of each key and its location shows how frequently the key changes and the extremely distant relationship of some adjacent keys.

Bar Number	Key
184	B minor
190	C major
194	C minor
195	E flat major
200	E flat minor
202	G flat major (F sharp)
204	A flat major
206	F minor
208	G minor

At this point the keys stop shifting in seconds and thirds and instead move through the circle of fifths.

Bar Number	Key
211	C minor
213	F minor
215	B flat major
217	E flat major
219	B flat major
220	F minor

The key then shifts to G minor in bar 222 and there follows a passage that would be a perfectly normal retransition, if only the piece were in the key of G. At the last moment there is a sudden shift to B flat, and the orchestra starts the recapitulation with the first theme in bar 235. The second part of the first theme follows and again is played by both the orchestra and the soloist. The transition is changed somewhat, but ends with the same half cadence in the key of B flat. The second theme group is now in the tonic key, with part one (bar 262)[6] again minor, the mode shifting to tonic major for part two (bar 275). Part three follows

[6] Several printed editions of this concerto have only nine measures between the bars marked 230 and 240. In these editions, all the numbers that follow are misplaced by one measure.

in bar 285, and part four in bar 298. The first half of the closing theme from the second exposition is followed in turn by parts one and two of the closing theme from the first exposition, thus recapitulating the material from both expositions. The orchestra next plays a typical approach to a cadenza, ending on a tonic six-four chord. After the cadenza there follows the second half of the closing theme of the second exposition, and then, to end the movement, the third part of the closing theme from the first exposition. Here is another example of the practice of rearranging the material from the exposition to produce a coda-like passage which actually uses no new material.

EXAMPLES FOR ANALYSIS

ABRIDGED SONATA FORM

Beethoven: *Piano Sonata No. 5, Op. 10, No. 1—2nd Movement*

Beethoven: *Symphony No. 8, Op. 93—2nd Movement*

Mozart: *Symphony No. 39, K. 543—2nd Movement*

Rossini: *Overture to the Barber of Seville*

SONATA-RONDO FORM

Beethoven: *Piano Sonata No. 8, Op. 13—Finale*

Beethoven: *Piano Sonata No. 15, Op. 28—Finale*

Beethoven: *Violin Concerto, Op. 61*

Mozart: *Piano Sonata in D, K. 576—Finale* (Mozart's variant of this form)

Mozart: *Piano Concerto No. 27 in B Flat, K. 595—Finale* (Mozart's variant)

Brahms: *Piano Concerto No. 2 in B Flat, Op. 83—Finale*

DOUBLE EXPOSITION IN CONCERTO

Any Classic or Romantic concerto that starts with a long passage for the orchestra alone probably uses this form. The concertos of Mozart seem the best introduction to this form. After several concertos with a double-exposition first movement have been studied, one that does not use this form, such as Mendelssohn's *Violin Concerto*, might be studied with profit.

VI

Vocal Music

IT IS NECESSARY to consider music written for voices apart from music written for instruments. The forms studied so far have been illustrated with examples from instrumental music with several different performance media used for each form. It is evident that each of these forms was suitable for a variety of media, and conversely, that performance medium has little basic influence on overall form. This is not true of vocal music, for vocal music is a combination of the arts of music and literature, and it is this dual aspect that must be considered whenever the form of a vocal piece is studied. In almost all instances the words existed before the music, and it is the text that gives rise to every aspect of the music. Thus a consideration of the effect of the text on the form is of great importance. With the exception of certain works like operas, vocal music uses texts that were not originally intended to be set to music. Hence most vocal texts have a formal structure of their own to which the form of the music is added. In adding the music the composer may alter or adapt the text, but in any case, he takes the final responsibility for the completed work of art, and it is his name that is primarily associated with it. Composers' judgments differ on the degree to which it is suitable to alter the form of the text—some prefer to keep the text exactly as they found it, and others abridge it and rearrange it quite freely.

As a start in the study of vocal music, we must consider the basic techniques of setting words to music, for these have a direct bearing on the form of vocal music. Rhythm is a basic element not only of music, but of the literary art as well, particularly poetry. So it is that the composer finds in the text a suggestion of the rhythms to be used. A slavish adherence to these rhythms will not do, for the rhythmic patterns of poetry, and to some extent of prose, are too limited to be of much value as rhythms in music. Indeed, the regular rhythm of poetry is more comparable to the meter of a piece of music than to its actual rhythmic pattern. This is not surprising, since in poetry the expression is far less dependant on the rhythmic element than is the case in music. This means that the composer must use a far greater variety of rhythms than he finds in his text if there is to be any variety and expression to the music. Almost any rhythmic pattern is possible, so long as the accents of the text and the strong and weak relationship between words or syllables is preserved. Strong syllables are set either with notes that are metrically stronger or with longer notes, the latter technique being especially appropriate for those languages in which stressed syllables of speech are prolonged rather than accented. Prose does not have the rhythmic monotony of poetry, but the rhythmic patterns of prose are often so varied and unrelated that they would not have much expressive value as music. Here again the composer uses a varied but organized musical rhythm that supports the underlying text rhythms without following them slavishly. A further source of rhythmic variety and expressiveness is the use of two or more notes of different pitches to set a single syllable, called a *melisma*. This gives greater emphasis to the syllable so set, not only because it occupies more time but because of the melodic expression of the melisma. Melismas are also useful to prolong a short text which, if set with one note to each syllable, would not occupy enough space to be important. A short text can also be stretched by repetition, or by a combination of repetition and melismas. An opposite problem is created by a text that is very wordy, and this calls for the composer to use *syllabic* style (one note per syllable) and rapid notes to the degree appropriate. The syllabic and melismatic techniques are nowhere better illustrated and contrasted in the same work than in the *Kyrie* and *Credo* in any setting of the Mass. A reading of these two texts will show how severe the problem is, since both sections are of equal importance to the service and demand treatments of equal scope.

Another problem that occurs when the literary art is combined with music arises from the fact that sung words progress more slowly than the same words spoken or read. This means that the composer is necessarily changing the pace of the text as he sets it to music, and while this does not change its formal proportions, it does affect the intentions of the author. This makes it desirable that the text be relatively short, and the composer may find it desirable to make abridgments or to use selections. This problem of the slow pace of sung words is especially acute in opera, since not only are the speeches of the characters prolonged, but the action is slowed by the length of time that it takes to present any verbal idea. The librettist of an opera must be especially aware of the problems and design this libretto accordingly. It is for this reason that operas are not plays set to music in their original form but rather use specially designed librettos.

Throughout the study of vocal music, the meaning and form of the text must be considered as one facet of the work being analyzed. This poses a problem of language. Vocal music in a foreign language should be studied with the aid of a translation, but it should be noted that many translations stress singability and the preservation of the original rhythms, and the exact order of words and their coincidence with the music may be slightly altered. Thus, if one spot in the music exactly sets the meaning of a single word or short phrase, the translation may not preserve this relationship, and the motivation of the music will be lost to the analyst unless the original text is considered. The problem is less acute if the music only creates the general mood of the text and does not attempt to reflect shades of meaning of special words, but the text must never be ignored in any consideration of vocal music. The first type of vocal music to be studied will be songs, since these are the simplest form and do not present the choral problem of imitative use of text.

SONGS AND THE SONG CYCLE

Vocal pieces and movements of vocal works tend to be shorter than their counterparts in instrumental music. It is difficult to say why this is. Perhaps it is that the voice tires more easily and therefore needs frequent pauses between numbers. Perhaps composers have found the rapid shifts of mood that accompany a series of short numbers more satisfactory for vocal music. Perhaps it is a result of the sort of text chosen, or perhaps the setting of the text is so important that a complex form with much development would detract from it.

Whatever the reason, songs tend to be rather short and so use shorter forms. From the time of the Classic Era the binary form has fallen into disuse, and since most texts are not suitable for rondo, the form most used for songs is the ternary form. Clearly this form has no equivalent in poetry, and the composer must therefore manipulate his text. Either the music of the first section must be returned with different words to make the last part of the form, or the words of the opening stanza must be returned literally at the end, in which case a large segment of the poem is repeated and the song ends at the poem's midpoint. Both of these techniques are used regularly by composers to write songs in ternary form, demonstrating to what extent musical considerations dominate song composition. In addition to the previously studied forms, two forms are commonly used for songs that have no counterpart in instrumental music. Each of these is so closely related to a use of the text that instrumental music, which has no text, cannot employ them. If the listeners have no understanding of the language of the words, the effect is very like that of instrumental music, a fact that poses great problems for the performance of vocal music. The problem is intensified by the fact that these two forms are very commonly used.

The first of these purely vocal forms is the *through-composed* song. In this form the music for each stanza of the poem is somehow different, and no later stanza is set with music that is a recapitulation of the music of any earlier stanza. This eliminates the basic formal principle of departure and return and removes the unifying factors found in the forms studied so far. Although this formal plan makes for a less successful musical structure, much of the formal strength is furnished by the design of the poem. The music is designed to follow the phrases and words of the poem rather closely and to set and amplify details of the poem, leaving the creation of the general design in the hands of the poet. Certain purely musical techniques of design are used in a through-composed song, the most important of these being tonality; if the song is extensive there will be a tonal arch.

The second of these purely song forms is the *strophic* song. In this form, identical music is used to set each stanza of a poem. Since the music for one stanza, or *strophe*, is quite short, it is usually through-composed. Strophic songs are sometimes varied by having a series of verses, each followed by a short refrain which is the same each time. This is more common in simple folk songs than in art music. Sometimes variety is achieved by setting a stanza to the same music but using the opposite mode. A good example of this is *Vergebliches Standchen* by Brahms, and an examination of the song will show why this change of mode is necessary to the text.

When a composer of songs wishes to write a longer and more complex work than a single song, he does not write a long complex song in a highly developmental style, but rather a group of songs called a *song cycle*. The songs of a cycle are related by a common theme or story and are meant to be sung as a unit, just as are the movements of an instrumental work. In spite of this, most song cycles contain one or more songs that have achieved greater popularity than the rest of the cycle and which are often performed singly. This practice of removing one song from a cycle is possible because each song has a form complete within itself, again like a movement of an instrumental work. The poems of the text may have been written to be heard as a group, in the manner of the cycle that we are to study, or they may be poems on a common subject assembled by the composer. In the latter case, they may not all be by the same author. A complete cycle provides a good study of songs, since not only can the structure of the cycle itself be studied, but also the structure of the individual songs. These will offer considerable variety, since it would be undesirable for all the movements of a single work to have identical forms.

The songs to be studied are for voice and piano, but the observations made about this medium are generally also true for voice with other types of accompaniment. It should be kept in mind that the medium used is not one in which there are parts of equal importance, since the voice has the words, and it is the poem that has been the starting point of the song. Also, although it is not satisfactory for the voice to be used for extended periods without any accompaniment, it is necessary that the piano be used alone at times to rest the voice and to provide sections where the expression is purely musical. Typical uses of the piano are as an introduction, a conclusion, and an interlude during the song. Notice the variety of Schumann's uses of the piano in this cycle.

Schumann: *Frauen Liebe und-Leben, Op. 42*

The eight songs of this cycle follow the course of the love and life of a woman. Each song describes a single event, spanning the emotional range from happy to tragic, and as such each song is an entity in itself. The songs will be discussed individually before the structure of the entire cycle is considered. As the songs are studied it is imperative to consult a score that offers a translation so that the meaning of the text can be clearly understood.

Seit ich ihn gesehen: This is a simple strophic song with two verses. The piano plays an introduction that consists of the first bar of the vocal melody and an interlude between the two verses that is the last fragment of the vocal melody. The melody itself is through-composed, and some fragments of it occur more than once, either being repeated literally or in sequence. This is typical of through-composed songs—while the term means that no long section will be repeated literally, some degree of unity of material is achieved and each new measure is not completely different from every preceding measure. After the second verse the piano again reiterates the end of the voice part and ends the song with the material from the very first bar, thus rounding out the form.

Er, der Herrlichste von Allen: This song is in the form of a rondo. The text is not the same for the second appearance of the rondo theme, but for its last appearance the opening stanza of the poem returns. The repeated-chord accompaniment starts in the piano and in the second bar the singer enters with the rondo theme, which is eight bars long. This theme is repeated literally to set the second stanza of the poem. In bar 9 the piano plays the beginning of the rondo theme with the first note delayed to make a syncopation, and in bar 17 this figure is the basis for a short piano interlude before the first episode, which starts in bar 21. Several secondary dominants create the feeling of moving from the tonic key in this episode, but a new key is never firmly established. The text of this episode is the third stanza of the poem, and the second appearance of the rondo theme, which follows in bar 29, provides a setting for the fourth stanza. The rondo theme is heard only once here, but it is extended two bars by reiterating the cadence to achieve a more final ending in E flat, the tonic key. This extension repeats the words of the previous two bars, and is used here as much to emphasize these words as to make a strong cadence. The second episode, which extends from bar 39 to bar 54, provides the setting for two more stanzas of the poem. Here the key center is in a state of flux, never settling in one key long enough to establish it firmly, and by the end of the episode in bar 54, a cadence is reached on an A major chord, a remote key for a song in E flat. The piano interlude that follows uses the form of the beginning of the rondo theme that was found in bar 17, and the harmony is a series of dominants. Schuman adds a G to the A major chord in bar 54 to make a dominant of the key of D. In bar 55 the D chord becomes the dominant of G, and so on—dominant of C in 56, of F in 57, of B flat in 58, and of E flat in 59. Finally, at bar 60, this chain of dominants comes to rest on an E flat tonic triad. The singer has entered in bar 57 with the rondo theme, the beginning of which is altered to accommodate the harmonic pattern of this passage. The text of this last appearance of the rondo theme is the first stanza of the poem. At the beginning and end of the song the piano is used alone, and during the song there are piano interludes beginning in bars 9, 17, and 54. Each time the same melodic material is used, which is a very common device which gives unity to the piano's participation in the song.

Ich kann's nicht fassen, nicht glauben: This poem is set as a ternary form, but Schumann does not use the obvious distribution of the text—using one stanza for each section of the form. Rather he uses the first stanza in section A, the next two stanzas in section B, and the opening stanza for the return of the A section, hence emphasizing this stanza. The middle section of this ternary form divides into two parts between bars 36 and 37, a division which coincides with the break between the second and third stanzas of the poem. Notice in all these songs how clearly Schumann retains the stanza structure of the original poem so that the song enhances and amplifies the poem but does not hide or destroy its structure. The middle section of the ternary form moves to the relative major, and there is a shift of mood, no doubt motivated by Schumann's desire to delineate the section of the poem that describes the singer's remembrances of moments with her loved one. With the return of the A section, the singer reiterates her surprise and joy at his love. In the coda, which starts in bar 68, the piano first plays a version of the first theme, and then the singer repeats the first two lines of the poem. Schumann's emphasis on these two lines illustrates how the composer of a song can manipulate the form and meaning of the poem as created by the poet.

Du Ring an meinem Finger: This is the best loved of the songs in this cycle and the one most likely to be heard by itself. The poem that serves as the text of this song has five stanzas, the first and last of which are identical. Since the third stanza has the same first line as the first and last stanzas, the alternate stanzas are similar. Schumann's use of the rondo form is a natural outgrowth of the poetic rondo already used for the text. The five sections of the form, each of which uses one stanza of the poem, start in bars 1, 9, 17, 25 and 33. The first two appearances of the rondo theme are identical, but the third appearance has the last two bars slightly altered to eliminate the cadence in the dominant that ended the first two. All three appearances of the rondo theme are each eight bars long, as are the two episodes. The singer actually starts a moment before the piano and there are no piano interludes, but the piano is heard alone at the end of the song. Neither episode really leaves the tonic key, although the second contains that same restless approach to tonal motion found in the second episode of the second song.

Helft mir, ihr Schwestern: This poem contains five stanzas. Again Schumann creates a structure based on the form of the poem. Here, too, the similarities of the beginnings of the first, third, and fifth stanzas influence the form, but the solution is different from that used in the previous song. After a two-bar piano introduction using the accompaniment of the vocal line, the singer enters with a melody that sets the first two stanzas of the poem, this section ending in bar 18. In bar 19, the vocal line which opened the song is used for the start of the third stanza, and what follows is basically the second strophe of a strophic song, although a comparison of bars 19 to 35 with bars 3 to 18 will reveal some melodic differences, reflecting the meaning of the third and fourth stanzas. In bar 37 the singer starts a third strophe, but this is shorter since it contains only one stanza. In bar 41 there is a sudden change in the mood of the music which cannot be explained in purely musical terms, but is rather a reflection of the bride's sorrow as she thinks of leaving her sisters.

The song ends with an extended piano postlude that is in the nature of a little march. Several of the songs that we have seen end with an elaborate piano passage after the singer has completed the vocal part of the song. Thus Schumann creates an expectation of this piano ending which reaches its fulfillment in the last song, by which time the listener will have become accustomed to closing interludes, so that the unusual length of the final piano postlude will not seem out of character with the preceding songs.

Süsser Freund, du blickest: In this song the young wife reveals to her husband the supremely happy news that they are to have a child. The first two stanzas of the poem serve as a prelude to the telling, ending with the statement that she will whisper in his ear. The piano interlude, which follows in bars 21 to 24, represents the whispered news. The third stanza reveals to us that the husband knows now what she wanted to tell him. Such a pause must come musically at an important juncture of the form, and such is the case here. The song is a ternary form, and this piano interlude occurs at the break between the A and B sections. This means that there is not a symmetric distribution of the poem, since the first two stanzas are contained in section A, the third stanza in section B, and the fourth stanza in the second A section. To accommodate two stanzas in the first section, Schumann uses the melody of this section twice, and uses it only once in the second A section. The melody of the A section ends inconclusively. To give a finality to the song, Schumann uses the expected piano postlude, but varies the procedure by once more having the singer sing the last words of the next-to-last line of the stanza, "dein Bildniss!" ("your image"). The very clear shift of mood that comes with the B section of this ternary form is accomplished in part by a shift of key to the subdominant. Tonic of course returns with the return of A.

An meinem Herzen, an meiner Brust: This four-stanza poem is set as a strophic song. The first three verses are similar, but the fourth, which portrays the new mother's increasingly animated joy, is so much faster that the rhythm of the accompaniment must be simplified. In addition, the music is changed in the last verse to achieve a climax, after which a calm piano postlude ends the song.

Nun hast du mir den ersten Schmerz getan: The woman's contemplation of her husband's death presents a great contrast of mood with the joy of the previous song, a contrast which is amplified musically by the shift in mode from D major to D minor and by the intense, almost declamatory style of this song. This style is in part made possible because the song is through-composed. Each new phrase evokes a powerful musical expression created for it alone. The song is a dramatic example of the effect that through-composition can achieve. The singer's final note is on a half cadence expressing a feeling, not of the finality of the death of her beloved, but of a continuing life. Then, in the most masterful touch in the entire song cycle, Schumann has the piano return the melody of the first song, as if to recall the memories of the first awareness of their love. This long conclusion in the piano has been foreshadowed by the piano postludes to previous songs and here seems inevitable. Schumann thus makes a rounded form of the cycle, but also it makes it very undesirable to perform this song by itself since the last half has no meaning if the first song, and indeed the entire cycle, is not heard with it.

In considering the form of the cycle as a whole, the pattern of keys of the successive songs is important. Example 72, page 100, shows these keys and their relation to tonic and to one another.

The end of the key pattern is particularly important to the cycle's expressiveness. The seventh song is in the key of D major, and as was previously noted the shift to D minor for the last song expresses its tragedy. At the same time D minor is a major third above the tonic key of B flat, so that for the return of the melody of the first song in the piano, the key can shift from D minor down a major third to B flat major, a key relationship which produces a calm, placid effect. In addition to the strength of design of the key pattern, the various songs have a complementary effect which contributes to their feeling of unity. Successive songs are rarely in the same mood or tempo, and there is a nice balance between their different moods. Clearly this and much else that contributes to the unity of this cycle stem from the poems themselves; but whatever the cause, this cycle gives as much evidence of being a unified design as any multimovement instrumental piece.

FORM IN OTHER VOCAL COMPOSITIONS

The previous discussion of form in songs and of the relationship of text to design has a bearing on form in all vocal music. Because of the great influence of the text, it is difficult to make meaningful generalizations about vocal music, particularly in view of its great

EXAMPLE 72: Schumann: *Frauen Liebe und-Leben, Op. 42*

Song	Form	Key	Relation to Tonic Key of Cycle and to Key of Other Songs
Seit ich ihn gesehen	Strophic	B flat	Tonic key of cycle
Er, der Herrlichste von Allen	Rondo	E flat	Subdominant key
Ich kann's nicht fassen, nicht glauben	Ternary	C minor	Relative minor of subdominant, the key of the previous song
Du Ring an meinem Finger	Rondo	E flat	Subdominant key returns
Helft mir, ihr Schwestern	Strophic	B flat	Tonic key returns
Süsser Freund, du blickest	Ternary	G major	A more remote key than previously used
An meinem Herzen, an meiner Brust	Strophic	D major	Dominant of the previous key
Nun hast du mir den ersten Schmerz getan	Through-composed	D minor	Parallel minor of the previous key
		B flat	Tonic key of cycle

variety and long history. All that is possible is a brief discussion of form as found in the more common types of vocal music. It should be noted that the classes of vocal music discussed are mainly differentiated by the text used, not by the form of the music.

If a text has a great many words and if it is necessary that these words be clearly understood by the listener, the composer will use *recitative*. This is a type of vocal passage in which the singer sings a text which may be prose or poetry, in a manner designed to imitate speech, using free rhythms in a declamatory style. Recitative is generally through-composed and accompanied by occasional chords or some such simple setting. A type of texture midway between recitative and song is *arioso*. This, too, is generally through-composed, or at least lacks the formal complexity of an aria.

An *aria* is a song and frequently uses the forms of songs previously studied [1], the name *aria* being used because of the type of work in which the song is found. A particularly common form used for arias in the Baroque Era was a ternary form in which only the first two parts were written out and the third part was produced by repeating the first part as a da capo. From this practice the form takes the name of *da capo aria*. Many da capo arias have a complex structure within each section of the ternary form and many are compound ternary forms.

In this century there has developed another way of using the voice that serves the same general function as recitative. This is *sprechstimme*, which is notated with a small cross in the stem of each note as seen in Example 73. The effect called for is midway between speech and song, and the singer follows the pitches only approximately, gliding from note to note.

EXAMPLE 73:   Schoenberg: *Pierrot Lunaire, Op. 21, No. 1—Mondestrunken*

[1] One other form used commonly for arias, the ritornello form, will be studied in Chapter VIII, and vocal examples of it will be seen at that time.

Vocal Music   101

When several parts are used, either in pieces for a group of soloists, or in choral music, the same words of the text may not appear in all the parts at the same time. This may lead to a complex overlapping of different parts of the text and may make it impossible to relate the music at any one point to a phrase or specific word of the text. In these cases the text will influence only the general nature of the passage, and the details of the form will be motivated by purely musical considerations. In a sense this is more like the procedures in instrumental music, and the observations about the motivating force of the text made previously are less true if the presentation of the text is so complex that it is not heard clearly. Complex choral passages often make use of much text repetition, as if to compensate for the difficulty of hearing the words. This is another way in which a long vocal work may grow out of a short text.

MASS AND REQUIEM

A musical setting of the Mass takes its general form from the basic parts of the Mass: the *Kyrie*, the *Gloria*, the *Credo*, the *Sanctus*, and the *Agnus Dei*. Most often these are each written as a movement, but a single section is sometimes the basis for several movements, a practice which began in the Baroque Era. The text of the *Kyrie* lends itself well to ternary form, and in the *Sanctus* the setting of the first *Hosanna* may be used for the second *Hosanna* as well. Beyond this, it is impossible to generalize on the forms used by composers for the sections of the Mass. The Requiem Mass differs in that the Introit *Requiem Aeternam* is set to music, the joyful *Gloria* and *Credo* are omitted, and the sequence *Dies Irae* is added. Long complex Requiem Masses may also break one part up into several movements, this being especially true of the *Dies Irae*. In this case the same music will return with every appearance of *Dies Irae*.

ORATORIO

This is a large religious work for soloists, chorus, and orchestra. The text is of a narrative nature and sometimes uses a soloist who serves as narrator. In form there are a large number of movements —some arias, some duets, trios, and quartets for the soloists, and some choral numbers. In addition, there is usually an instrumental overture, and there may be other movements for orchestra alone during the work. If an oratorio is long, it will be divided into several large sections, each of which consists of a number of movements. Each part will deal with some aspect of the story, and will be musically complete in itself, similar to an act of an opera. Recitatives are used to carry the action along more quickly, while the arias, which tend to slow the action, are used to highlight or emphasize particularly dramatic moments. Further emphasis is also provided by ensemble numbers and choral numbers. Since there are many movements to such a work, no one movement is too long. The vocal forms previously studied and the ritornello form are the typical structures used in such a work.

CANTATA

This may be religious or secular and is a work of smaller scope than an oratorio. Soloists, chorus, and orchestra may be employed, but many cantatas use more limited resources. Some are written for one or two singers with accompanying small orchestra or simply with continuo. Like oratorios cantatas have several movements of the type previously discussed, but in so small a piece there is no division into parts. J. S. Bach was fond of a type of cantata based upon a Lutheran chorale. This type is treated in the chapter on variations.

In addition to these general categories, there are many shorter choral pieces about which it is impossible to generalize. These are usually relatively simple in form, and frequently make use of imitation. A study of these choral pieces—madrigals, motets, anthems, and many others—depends upon a consideration of individual examples. In addition, those such as the motet which have a long history have changed in form from era to era, a fact that complicates any generalizations. Whatever the work studied, the ever-present interrelation of text and music is a prime factor in the form and must be a part of any significant analysis.

OPERA

In opera music is combined not only with words, but also with drama and sometimes with dance. Any study of form in opera must take into account all of the art forms represented. Such an analysis is necessarily complex. As was mentioned previously, an opera uses as its text a libretto which is especially written or adapted for this purpose. The most basic formal divisions in an opera are those of the drama, that is, the division into acts and scenes.

The older form of opera, and one used occasionally to the present day, makes use of a series of set musical pieces within an act or scene. Each of these is formally complete in itself, and these numbers may follow one another in continuous succession or be interspersed with dialogue. This dialogue, which does the most to further the dramatic action, is usually sung as recitative, but it may be spoken. In solo arias, duets or other ensemble numbers for the principals, chorus numbers, or dance numbers the various small forms commonly used for vocal music are found, and each of these numbers is complete in itself and could be performed separately from the opera. The orchestra usually plays an overture or prelude before the first act, which often makes use of sonata form or abridged sonata form. The overture may be based on themes from the opera itself. Many times this is not the case, and the overture's only connection with the opera is that it sets the general mood of the opera or of the opening scene. The orchestra may also play preludes to the other acts or interludes between acts or related scenes, especially when a complex shift of scenery is necessary.

Since all of these numbers are relatively short, an opera may consist of forty or fifty different numbers. To counteract the disconnected effect of so many separate pieces, composers sometimes connect several of them with a continuous flow of music. This technique is especially common in the finale of an act and allows the act to end with a continuous sweep of music and thus achieve a greater dramatic climax. Such finales or other extended sections are readily divisible into several subsections, and these in turn commonly use the forms mentioned previously.

In the later operas of Richard Wagner there is a new approach to form in opera. While the beginnings of these concepts can be seen in earlier operas, their final development is largely the work of Wagner. This new approach to opera did not supplant the older type just described, and to this day both types are written. Alban Berg's *Wozzeck* uses Wagner's techniques, and *The Rake's Progress* of Stravinsky is based on the traditional separate numbers. In the Wagner type of opera the music for one act or scene is a continuous flow, and the only large divisions of the music come at the end of a scene. There are no separate arias or other numbers, but rather the whole is fused into a large musical structure not unlike the movement of a symphony. However, the large forms commonly used to write long instrumental works are not suitable for a complete scene of an opera, since the chances of the form of the dramatic action coinciding with the usual areas of the instrumental forms are exceedingly remote.[2]

Since it is impossible that a passage of music as long as an act of an opera should be one section, the composer takes advantage of whatever divisions are in the libretto to subdivide the music. Divisions into small scenes between characters, specific events of the action, and the like make it possible for the composer to cast his music into the series of sections so necessary for large pieces. Because the beginnings and endings of these sections are identifiable both in the music and in the action, each seems a product of the other. Moreover, a character in the opera may have a long speech which will enable the composer to write a solo musical number that is the equivalent of an aria in the older style. The fact that these arias can be done as separate numbers in concert programs demonstrates to what extent they are complete and separate forms.

The continuous flow of music desired for this type of opera is achieved despite these self-sufficient sections by employing transitional music between them which avoids final-sounding cadences and pauses that would break the flow of the music. One important characteristic of this type of opera is the use of the process of development. Since the freer structure of developmental sections does not demand specific sections at specific places, it enables the composer to move freely as the drama progresses. The developmental process makes use of themes and motives, and in opera these must have dramatic significance. Wagner evolved the technique of using a relatively small number of motives or themes associated with specific characters, objects, events in the drama, or ideas. Development, transformation, or any other use of these motives contributes to the drama of the opera. Formal structure, motivic structure, and development are easily perceived in such an opera, but it is impossible to generalize about these techniques, since the practices of a particular opera are derived from the speeches and

[2] A highly successful exception to this statement is Berg's opera *Wozzeck*, which makes use of a complete instrumental form for each scene, yet preserves a close relationship between the music and the drama.

actions of the characters. A specific application of these techniques can be illustrated by a brief analysis of one act from an opera in which the music is a continuously flowing, unified structure.

Puccini: *La Bohème—Act I*

It is presupposed in all the analyses in this book that the reader will become familiar with the sound of each piece discussed so that the analysis can be related to the actual music. In this case, hearing the music presents only one aspect of this work, since it is intended to be seen as a production in a theatre. If it is not possible to actually see *La Bohème* staged, the music and a score (with English translation) should be studied carefully in the light of this analysis, and special attention should be given to the action and staging of the drama. The act is based on a small number of melodic ideas, which are given names in the analysis. These names are used for identification purposes only, and should not be regarded as an interpretation of the meaning of the opera, which is best understood from the music and action itself. The dramatic subtleties of the opera far transcend any labels.

Example 74 is a chart of the form of the entire first act of the opera. The divisions of the form are indicated, and the principal themes and key centers are identified. The themes within each section are identified as theme A, B, and C and since the same letters are used for the themes of each section, it is necessary to identify a theme by scene as well as by letter designation. The key centers given are the main ones, and in cases where rapid modulations occur and no key is more important than another, the key is listed as shifting. It is desirable that this diagram be consulted throughout this analysis.

Although the music for this act flows continuously, the act is a series of sections. These divisions are present in the action of the drama, and Puccini has made the music support the existence of these sections so that there is one over-all pattern to the form of both the drama and the music. As is the case in many long works of absolute music, the form is divided on several levels, large sections consisting in turn of smaller sections. The form must be first discussed in terms of the largest section before the structure of each section is considered. The act is divided into two halves which are almost the equivalent of two scenes, but the action and music flow continuously from one to the other. The first half of the act intro-

EXAMPLE 74: Puccini: *La Bohème—Act I*

First Half of the Act: The Bohemians at Home

SCENE AND STAGE ACTION	OPENING SCENE			SECOND SCENE: THE BOHEMIANS CELEBRATE				SCENE WITH THE LANDLORD				THE BOHEMIANS LEAVE FOR THE CAFÉ	
MUSICAL THEME	A	B	A, B, & new melodies developed	A B	B	A	A & B developed	A A	B	A	C	B of opening scene	A of opening scene
KEY CENTER	C	B flat shifting	shifting	D	E flat shifting	shifting	D	F	G flat; C sharp minor	D flat	B minor & shifting	G flat	G flat

Second Half of the Act: Rudolfo meets Mimi

SCENE AND STAGE ACTION	FIRST MEETING AND DUET		RUDOLFO'S ARIA			MIMI'S ARIA						INTERLUDE, BOHEMIANS RETURN	DUET: RUDOLFO AND MIMI	
MUSICAL THEME	A	B	A	B	C	A	B	A	C	D	B	A of opening scene	C from Rudolfo's Aria	A from Rudolfo's Aria
KEY CENTER	B & G	B flat	D flat	F & A flat	A flat	D	D	D	D	D	B	G	A	C

duces us to the Bohemians and their way of life, and comes to an end when all but Rudolfo leave for the Café. The second half starts with the appearance of Mimi, and progresses to her final duet with Rudolfo. This division of the act is based on the action of the drama, but it will be seen that if the music were to be considered by itself, it too would divide into the same two parts. Since this is true of all the sections, the division into sections will be discussed in terms of the action. However it should be observed that the music is always similarly divided in terms of themes, key centers, and all the elements that give music the sense of a series of sections. Having now established the two halves of the act we shall consider them one at a time.

The scene with the Bohemians lasts from the beginning of the act to number 25 and is divided into four sections.[3] The first of these presents Rudolfo and Marcello on Christmas Eve, cold and hungry and without the money to remedy the situation. The second section begins at number 10 with the arrival of Colline who brings firewood, food, and money. These two sections are natural ones in the drama, for it was the intention of Puccini and the librettists to depict the contrast between the joy of the Bohemians when money and material comforts are to be had, and their despair when they are lacking. The third section is occasioned by the arrival of the landlord for the rent (number 17). This interrupts the festive scene, and this section lasts until the landlord retreats in confusion (number 22). The last section is the leave-taking of those who have decided to go to the Café. This leaves Rudolfo alone, and sets the stage for Mimi's entrance. The first half of the act comes to a complete halt before number 25, and the moment's pause and new start that follows gives the impression of a brief passage of time. Each section of this first half of the act can now be considered in detail.

The first two bars present a motive that is basic to the entire opera. It is always related to the Bohemians, and is used many times during the opera to suggest them and to set the mood of the entire opera. The melodic idea that is quoted with it in Example 75 comes from the fifth bar and is derived from the basic motive. This first section is based on the two themes which are quoted and labeled A and B in Example 75.

[3] Rehearsal numbers correspond to those in the editions of G. Ricordi and G. Shirmer.

EXAMPLE 75:   Puccini: *La Bohème, Act I*—Opening Scene

Theme A

Theme B

The initial motive is developed in many ways throughout the act, and this aspect of the composition should be studied carefully. The entire act is an exceedingly tightly-knit structure, as much so as many symphonies. Theme B is found first at the *Lo stesso movimento* between 1 and 2. Before 3, Theme A returns, and at number 3 there is a section like the opening of the act. At the *a tempo come prima* after 4, Theme B returns. This alteration of two themes is one of Puccini's favorite formal devices and is found throughout the act. The rest of this section is based on a combination of these two themes with two other new, but minor, themes. The shift in mood with the coming of food and wood at 10, which starts the second section, has already been mentioned. Puccini achieves this shift musically by introducing a new theme, one that is more joyful and exuberant than any heard before. This theme is truly representative of the joys of the Bohemian life shown in the

EXAMPLE 76:   Puccini: *La Bohème*—The Bohemians Celebrate

Theme A

Theme B

Theme C

Vocal Music   109

scene that follows. The themes of this section may be seen in Example 76. The first two themes are again used in an alternating fashion at 10, 12, after 12, and at 14, respectively.

After 14, A and B are combined and developed until 16, where theme C is introduced. The use of this new theme illustrates the extreme unity of the opera. Here it is a rather gentle setting for Schaunard's song about the delight of Christmas Eve in the Latin Quarter. At the beginning of the Second Act, when we are actually in the Latin Quarter a little later the same evening, this same theme is used, transformed into exciting and boisterous music. Just at the end of this section, at the *Tempo Primo* (*Allegro brillante*), Theme A of this section returns to round out the form and firmly establish the mood of celebration that is interrupted by the landlord's knock.

The scene with the landlord also uses three basic themes, which can be seen in Example 77. The first two are alternated in the manner of a ternary form, Theme A occuring at 18, Theme B at 19, and Theme A returning at 20, this time much shortened. Theme C occurs after 21, and a series of imitative entrances are used to set a passage of dialogue.

EXAMPLE 77: Puccini: *La Bohème*—Scene with the Landlord

Theme A

Theme B

Theme C

By courtesy of G. Ricordi & C., Milan, copyright owners.

The final section of this half of the act returns to the two main themes from the very first section, Theme B coming at 23 and Theme A at 24. The reprise of these themes rounds out this half, and, with the final-sounding ending before 25, makes this half of the act a musically complete unit.

The second half of the act also divides into four basic sections, as if to balance the four-part structure of the first half. These divisions, too, follow the action. The first is the scene in which Rudolfo and Mimi first meet. There follow two arias in which first Rudolfo and then Mimi tell more of themselves, and then, following a brief interruption by Rudolfo's impatient companions, Rudolfo and Mimi sing a duet which ends the act.

At 25 the orchestra plays a brief introduction which starts this section after the previous cadence and also sets a completely new mood. Mimi enters and converses with Rudolfo, against a musical background based on Theme A in Example 78. At 27 a more lyrical melody (Theme B) follows, and this is the basis for the rest of this conversation.

EXAMPLE 78:   Puccini: *La Bohème*—The Meeting of Rudolfo and Mimi

By courtesy of G. Ricordi & C., Milan, copyright owners.

At 30 the first of the two arias begins. These arias are the closest thing to the set pieces of the older style of opera found in this act, but the degree to which they are integrated into the fabric of the act becomes apparent when they are removed to be sung separately in concert. They possess neither a satisfactory start nor ending, since it was the composer's intention that, while they must be separate entities, they could not be so separate as to break the flow of the act. Rudolfo's aria, which extends from 30 to 35, uses the three themes shown in Example 79. In contrast to his previous practice, Puccini uses each of these themes only once. However, they are not quoted and left entirely, since two of them form the basis for the final section of the act. Theme A comes at 30, Theme B at 31, and Theme C after 32.

At 32 Theme B of the opening scene of the opera is heard. Mimi's aria, which follows directly, uses the four themes in Example 80. Some of these themes are returned to make an interesting rounded form: A B A C D B. These themes occur at 35 (A), 36 (B), after 36 (A), 37 (C), 38 (D), and after 38 (B).

EXAMPLE 79:   Puccini: *La Bohème*—Rudolfo's Aria

By courtesy of G. Ricordi & C., Milan, copyright owners.

EXAMPLE 80:   Puccini: *La Bohème*—Mimi's Aria

By courtesy of G. Ricordi & C., Milan, copyright owners.

In a brief interlude, at 39, the other Bohemians urge Rudolfo to hurry, and the opening motive of the opera is used, returning the mood of the first half of the act. At 41, after the others have been persuaded to go on ahead, Rudolfo and Mimi are left to sing the inevitable love duet. After 41 the first big climax is reached using the C theme of Rudolfo's aria, and after 43, Theme A of Rudolfo's aria is used for the climax that ends the act. Just after 43 a slight suggestion of the first theme of Mimi's aria is heard in the orchestra. The order of the two themes from Rudolfo's aria is inverted so that the act will end with the very first melody that he sang to Mimi. In the last act, this same theme is used in a very moving passage during the death of Mimi. The last part of the last act should be studied for the use of the themes that have been presented in this act to further demonstrate the thematic unity of this opera and also the dramatic power of these musical techniques.

EXAMPLES FOR ANALYSIS

The technique used in this chapter of studying both a song cycle and the structure of its individual songs is an excellent one. Simple cycles are *Die schöne Müllerin* of Schubert and the *Dichterliebe* of Schumann. More complex forms than those studied in this chapter can be seen in the *Four Serious Songs* of Brahms.

An investigation of opera might well start with a study of all or part of the other three acts of *La Bohème,* since many of the themes of this work are already familiar. A good place to start on the operas of Wagner is *Die Meistersinger von Nürnberg.* A contemporary example of continuous opera is Berg's *Wozzeck.* The number opera should be studied first in the operas of Mozart. An excellent contemporary example, and one that follows Mozart's techniques very closely, is *The Rake's Progress* of Stravinsky.

VII

Multimovement

Compositions

THE FORMS THAT have been discussed in the previous chapters may be used for the design of a complete piece if the piece contains only one movement. However, if a piece consists of two or more movements, these forms are not used for the piece as a whole. This chapter is concerned with the structure of multimovement compositions. The forms for single movements have been described in some detail, since these forms are based on a rather specific plan of design. The formal relationships within a movement can be demonstrated by an examination of tonal, thematic and motivic, and developmental relationships, and many other means. There is no correspondingly exact means of demonstrating the relationship between several movements of a composition. This is not to say that a complete composition has less unity than exists within its several movements, but only that the techniques used by composers to relate movements are more elusive and cannot be described as precisely.

The most easily studied device for organizing the several movements of a composition is tonality. This is both because this device has already been studied within a single movement and also because it is easily discernible. At times, indeed, tonal relationships provide the only obvious connection from movement to movement. However, care must be taken to avoid exaggerating the importance of the tonal structure, for it is but one of the means of creating unity. Just as a movement will have more than one key center, so a multimovement composition will have more than one key for its various movements. As in the case of a movement, the most typical key pattern is that of the tonal arch, with the first and last movements in the tonic key, and one or more of the intervening movements in some other key. In this case, the keys used are usually closely related, and ordinarily there is only one contrasting key before the tonic returns. It can be seen how critical it is that the tonic key of a movement be very clearly felt, since it is, in turn, creating the tonal pattern of the entire piece. It is impossible not to be aware of the relationship of keys, both within and between movements. The key pattern for a single movement must not only be worked out in relation to the structure of the movement, but also in relation to the key patterns within other movements of the composition.

Tonal practices are easy to see, but there is much more to the organization of a multimovement composition than the tonal scheme. Perhaps a negative example will serve to illustrate this statement. Beethoven wrote two symphonies in the key of F major. Approaching them solely from the standpoint of key, one could suggest playing the first four movements of the *Sixth* followed by the finale of the *Eighth*. While it is true that either finale would serve equally well to complete the F major tonal arch, the suggestion is none the less ludicrous. Yet if you consider thematic relationships, neither movement has a single theme or motive in common with any other movement of the two symphonies. Here, too, one movement seems as suitable for use as the other. However, other less tangible factors make the substitution impossible. The fourth movement of the *Sixth* is the agitated storm movement, and the finale that Beethoven wrote to follow it is calm and placid in contrast. The prevailing mood of the *Sixth Symphony* is one of extreme calm, a fact which is apparent even in the first few moments of the symphony. The proper finale preserves this mood and ends the work as it has begun. The active, excited finale of the *Eighth Symphony* is not at all in the mood needed to bring the *Sixth* to a proper close. The *Eighth Symphony* is one of Beethoven's most humorous works, and the finale is the lightest of the four movements. In its place, the movement is masterful, but used to end the *Sixth Symphony* its humor would be shocking and the movement would seem exceedingly crude, and not really very funny.

Of course the suggestion of switching movements between two Beethoven symphonies is preposterous, a fact readily felt without the foregoing discussion. The point is that there are forces which bind movements together that go beyond the easily discovered ones of key structure and thematic relationship. The fact that these forces are intangible and difficult to find and describe does not make them less real, and they exist as strongly for performers and listeners as they do for composers. In a piece of several movements, the composer has created a single work which is intended to be a whole and should be experienced as such. The performer plays the several movements together not merely in deference to the composer's wishes, but because he too understands that they are not separate entities, but rather subdivisions of a complete piece. This unity is so basic that it is only programs of a rather low musical level that contain many isolated movements instead of complete pieces. The listener also is a part of this practice. He listens attentively to the entire composition and does not interrupt it with applause. It may seem to the neophyte at a concert that the custom of not applauding between movements is an arbitrary one to trap the unwary, but in truth music is an art of sounds, and extraneous sounds between movements disturb the train of thought and hurt the enjoyment of the composition.

A basic source of unity within a multimovement work is the relationship of the mood and expression of the various movements, especially of adjacent movements. Here a contradictory pair of principles exist. On the one hand the movements of a work must be sufficiently similar in expression to seem parts of the same whole, yet on the other hand adjacent movements are usually unlike, even opposite, in nature. The attraction of opposites seems to be a basic factor in structure.

These contradictory statements can be clarified if discussed one at a time. In the previous consideration of the possibility of exchanging the movements of two Beethoven symphonies, the point was made that the *Sixth Symphony* had a prevailingly placid nature that demanded a finale of the proper mood. So it is with any composition of several movements—although the several movements are each individual, and unlike any other, there is still a prevailing expression in the work that dominates all the movements and to which they must conform. It matters not whether the over-all mood of the work is seen as the sum total of that of the movements, or as predetermined, with the expression of each movement conforming to it. In any case, this total expression does exist, and this relationship between each movement and the complete work is its product. The relationship is one of musical expression, and the fact that it does not translate well into words of technical analysis does not hide its existence from the listener.

At the same time, if each movement of a work were exactly like every other, there would be no need to hear the entire piece. Furthermore, no matter how effective the expression of a movement, its impact is greater if there is an adjacent movement of a completely opposite mood. Consider how much more exciting a fast movement is if it follows one that is calm, and how much more placid a slow movement is if it follows an agitated one. So it is that successive movements of a work are in a complementary relationship to one another. This relationship so heightens the effect of each movement that the movements seem necessary to one another, and there is actually the effect of unity due to an attraction of opposites. Thus a composition has a total mood and expression which is created by a series of movements that contrast with each other. The composer is constantly aware of this aspect of his composition, yet it is impossible to make a technical analysis beyond this general discussion, for such unity exists in the realm of expression and feeling, not in the technical realm.

THE SONATA-TYPE PIECE

This is a distinct type of multimovement work for which no general name exists. It is convenient to refer to this type of work as a *sonata*, but care must be taken that confusion does not exist between this and other uses of the term. The reason that there is no general name for this type of work is that it is variously known according to the performance medium for which it is written. Thus if it is written for piano or other keyboard instruments, or for a string or wind instrument combined with piano, it is known as a *sonata*. If it is written for a chamber group, the name varies according to the number of players and the medium: *duet, piano trio,*[1] *string quartet,*

[1] *Piano trio* means piano, violin, and cello, not three pianos. The medium is named from the odd instrument that is added to a group of string instruments, so that one also speaks of piano quartets, oboe quartets, clarinet quintets, etc. However, in the case of the wind instruments, four clarinets used together would also be called a clarinet quartet, so that the term is somewhat ambiguous.

woodwind quintet, etc. If a large instrumental group such as an orchestra or band is used, the piece is called a *symphony*, and if this same large group is used to accompany one or more soloists, it is termed a *concerto*. The lack of a single name for this general type of piece often leads to contradictions, such as the definition of a symphony as a sonata for orchestra. This is a perfectly good definition if *sonata* is understood to refer to the basic type of piece, not the work for solo instrument.

The basic form of the sonata type of piece developed from the Italian Overture of the Baroque Era and consists of three movements in the tempo relationship of fast – slow – fast. There are sometimes four movements instead of three, in which case the extra one is a dance movement. This dance movement is usually inserted between the slow movement and the finale, although it is sometimes found between the first two movements. In the eighteenth century the dance was a minuet, but after its introduction by Beethoven the scherzo became more common. There are also isolated instances of other dances such as waltzes and gavottes, as well as other types of music, such as the march. Brahms often substitutes an intermezzo-like movement for the more usual dance. Each movement of this type of work has a different nature and function, although generalizations about them can lead to an oversimplified picture of the structure of these compositions.

The first movement is usually a sonata form, and is basically a fast movement, although it may start with a slow introduction. In this case, the sonata form does not start until the main body of the movement, that is, until the fast tempo. In the eighteenth century and often in more recent times the introduction does not share thematic material with the sonata form that follows, but sometimes themes from the sonata form are presented, or at least hinted at, in the introduction. Most commonly it is the first theme that is anticipated. The main body of the first movement is relatively long in relation to the length of the piece and is complex and highly developmental. The first movement is characterized by great scope and variety of expression, and is the sort of movement that requires intense and careful listening if it is to be fully understood. Some modern sonata-type works do not use sonata form for the first movement, but whatever form is used will be intense and complex, thus leaving the general nature of the first movement unchanged. In modern pieces the slow introduction is more likely to be thematically related to some part of the piece that it introduces, and it may well be recapitulated later in the movement or in the piece.

The second movement offers a relief from the intense listening required by the first movement, since the tempo is slower and the listener has more time to absorb each detail of the form. Furthermore, slow movements tend to emphasize lyric melody rather than development; some of the most moving melodic writing is found in slow movements. The forms used vary. Sonata form is very common, and so is abridged sonata form, since it emphasizes the presentation of melodies rather than their development. Another attraction of the abridged form for slow movements is that it is shorter, a great advantage in a movement which moves at a slow pace. Simple rondo and sonata rondo are used, as are small forms such as ternary and compound ternary. Slow movements may also consist of a theme and variations, and actually many types of forms have proven useful for the composition of a slow movement.

If there is a dance movement, it is usually the third movement, although on occasion it may come between the first movement and the slow movement. The advantage of the usual arrangement is that the work ends with two faster movements instead of having two fast movements before the slow movement. When the dance movement is second, the first movement is very often slower, as in the *Ninth Symphony* of Beethoven. The fast dance movement is then put second to separate the moderate first movement from the slow movement, an illustration of the composer's desire not to have adjacent movements too similar. The dance movement is in a simple and direct form, usually a compound ternary, as if to offer a relief from the concentration needed for the first two movements.

In the finale the form chosen varies with the medium of the work, something that is true of no other movement. It is impossible to say why this is, and it is only true in general, but rondo finales are generally not found in symphonies and string quartets, although they are common in concertos and sonatas. All works of this type may use the sonata form for the finale, and there are also instances of the use of theme and variations, fugues, and other forms. The general description of the sonata-type composition spoke of the first and last movements as both being fast movements, and this is true in the sense that they are both faster than the slow movement. The finale, however, is generally faster and more climactic than the first movement, so that, as in a single movement, the greatest climax is reached near the end. The ebb and flow of the climaxes is an important aspect of the form of any multimovement work.

This discussion gives a brief description of the typical plan of the movements of a sonata-type work, and certain common variants must be described for the sake of completeness. First, the medium has some effect on whether there are four movements or three, that is, whether the dance-like movement is included. It is more often present in symphonies and string quartets, less commonly present in piano trios and sonatas, and rarely found in concertos. Another common variant is the writing of three movements that seem to be the last three movements of a typical four-movement work. Such a plan can be seen in Beethoven's *Piano Sonata in C Sharp Minor, Op. 27, No. 2* (Moonlight). The opening slow movement is like the typical second movement, and this is followed by a scherzo and a sonata-form finale. Thus the sonata is the usual four-movement plan abridged to omit the first movement. When the sonata-form first movement is left out, the composer usually writes the slow movement or the finale in sonata form, as if he owed the listener at least one such form. It is common in this abridged form to make the slow movement that starts the work a theme and variations, as in Beethoven's *Piano Sonata in A Flat, Op. 26*.

Some works have a pair of movements, but if they are both fast the second may well have a slow introduction to separate them. Such is the case with Beethoven's *Piano Sonata in C, Op. 53* (Waldstein). Sometimes there are more than the usual three or four movements. Beethoven exceeded four movements in several of his late quartets —the *Quartet in C Sharp Minor* actually contains seven. It should be noted that when such a large number of movements is used, they are not all very long, and some of the shorter ones do not really stand alone, but rather seem to be introductions to those that follow. Contemporary composers feel drawn to use more than four movements for a rather special reason. The original plan of the movements of the sonata type of piece was symmetric in that a slow movement was framed between two fast movements. The addition of a fourth movement disturbed this symmetry, and certain contemporary composers seek to reestablish the balance of the original plan. For this purpose an odd number of movements is used, so that the movements can radiate on either side of the middle movement. The *Concerto for Orchestra* of Bartók illustrates this practice. The first and fifth movements are both fast and both complex sonata forms. The second and fourth movements are more relaxed, both in form and in the music itself, the second featuring simple passages for pairs of instruments and the fourth being an intermezzo. In the center, and quite unlike any other movement, is the Elegy. Thus the basic plan is this:

First Movement	Second Movement	Third Movement	Fourth Movement	Fifth Movement
Fast and complex	Moderate and simple	Slow and somber	Moderate and simple	Fast and complex

A very similar plan is used by Bartók in his *Fifth String Quartet* except that here the middle movement is a scherzo and the second and fourth are slow movements. The first and last movements are not only fast and complex, but share the same main theme. Moreover, the first theme of the first movement is used in the coda of the last movement, thus linking the end of the quartet to the theme that opened it.

In a few sonata-type works two or more movements are grouped together and these larger groups are then combined. Sometimes this is achieved by connecting two movements so that the first does not come to a conclusive ending but rather flows directly into the second. Beethoven's *Fifth Piano Concerto* (Emperor), *Violin Concerto*, and *Triple Concerto* all illustrate this technique. In each work the first movement stands alone, but the second movement, in each a slow movement, breaks off before it ends and flows into a passage which is a transition to the last movement. The finale then follows directly, and the effect is almost one of a long movement in two distinctly different tempos. Not quite, however, since each movement does have its own complete form. The first movement of each concerto is so long that the second movement and finale combined are about its equal in length, a fact which also contributes to the impression that the concerto consists of two equal parts although it embodies the usual three movements. An interesting example of an organization into parts is furnished by the *Third Symphony* of William Schuman. Here the score is labeled to indicate two parts of two movements each, the first part a *Passacaglia* and *Fugue* and the second a *Chorale* and *Toccata*. The pause that one would expect between movements comes between the parts, and the two movements of a pair are connected. Another arrangement is found in Mahler's *Third Symphony* where there are two parts, the first part containing just the first movement, the second the other five.

As has just been suggested, movements are not always separated from one another by a pause, but may rather be connected. The Mendelssohn *Violin Concerto* has the usual three movements, but they are connected so that when the work is played, one long sweep of music results. At the end of the first movement the first bassoon holds a note, and one by one other woodwinds enter to make the first chord of the second movement. After the second movement, a brief interlude provides a bridge to the last movement. This is a common technique for connecting movements and is particularly common in the music of Stravinsky. In fact, the linking passage between the second and third movements in his *Symphony in Three Movements* is even labeled *Interlude*.

Individual movements of two complete works are analyzed in the course of this book, the *Seventh Symphony* of Beethoven and the *Octet* of Stravinsky. In Chapter X, the chapter on variations, the slow movement of the Stravinsky *Octet* is analyzed, and after this has been studied, the entire *Octet* should be examined in the light of this chapter. Notice that the second movement does not come to any satisfactory conclusion, but rather the fugue simply dissolves into the transition that leads to the rondo. Here, then, the first movement is one unit and the second and third movements are a second.

Since all four movements of the Beethoven *Seventh Symphony* have already been analyzed, we can consider the form of the entire symphony at this time.

Beethoven: *Symphony No. 7 in A, Op. 92*

The greatest factor in the unity of this symphony is its rhythmic, dance-like mood, which creates the feeling of the various movements belonging together that was mentioned earlier. This feeling that the four movements are united to serve a common expressive purpose is the basic source of the structural strength of the symphony, but while this is apparent in musical and artistic terms, this writer at least feels incapable of adequately treating the matter in words.

A second aspect of the design is readily discernible—the tonal plan of the symphony. The first movement is in A major, the key of the symphony. For the second movement the key shifts to A minor, although the use of A major for the key of the second theme might be again mentioned at this time, since it takes on added significance when it is viewed as the tonic key of the first movement. The third movement is in a most unusual key, F major, the major key a major third below the tonic key of the symphony. This key sounds as new and fresh here as an F major triad sounds when used as an altered submediant chord in the key of A major. The extensive use of the key of A, major and minor, dictates the use of a more unusual key for the scherzo. For the trio, the key again shifts down a third, this time to D major. Although this, in turn, is an unusual key to follow F major, it is the subdominant key of A, the tonic of the symphony. Thus two unusual key relationships, A to F and F to D, yield a common key, the subdominant. It is also worth noting that, since the slow movement was in the tonic minor, there has been no previous extended use of the subdominant key, and its use for the trio is even more important as utilizing one more key that is related to A major. The third movement closes in F, and the finale starts with the entire orchestra playing octave E's. These are followed by a dominant seventh chord on E which, in turn, leads to the tonic key of the finale, A major. Thus the finale is in the tonic key of the symphony, but the path into this key is very exciting because of the shift from the F major scherzo. Although the finale could be played by itself, the drama of this tonal motion would be lost.

The dance-like nature of the work is embodied in every movement, but it is especially dominant in the first movement, the scherzo, and the finale. In a sense, then, these movements are very similar, but there is still sufficient difference between them so that each movement preserves its individuality. One of the factors in this distinction is the meter. The finale has a duple subdivision of the beat and the other two a triple subdivision. Moreover, Beethoven's tempo markings suggest that the beat of the scherzo is faster than that of the first movement (104 versus 132).

In the analysis of the first movement, careful attention was given to the structure of the climaxes. As might be expected, the design of the climaxes is also an important factor in the structure of the entire symphony, and one that contributes much to its unity. The analysis of the climaxes given in Chapter IV will be continued to cover the entire symphony.

It was seen that the greatest climax of the first movement occurred at the very end of the movement, so it is not surprising that the second movement starts quietly and builds very slowly to a climax. After the first climax in bar 75, the movement subsides, and there is only one more climax in the entire movement, the one that comes with the return of the rondo theme in bar 214. This second climax is greater than the first, but neither reaches the height of intensity found in the first movement.

The scherzo starts at a high level of force. While the main body of the scherzo contains several climaxes, the highest point comes in the third section of the trio. Since the trio occurs twice, this same climax returns, which gives the scherzo two equal climaxes instead of the usual single one. This is possible because the scherzo is a movement of a longer work and is not intended to stand alone. Again, neither of these climaxes quite reaches the heights achieved in the first movement.

The finale starts immediately at a very high level, and by the third part of the first theme, the cumulative effect of so much driving motion is greater than the final climax of the first movement. Thus the finale asserts itself at once, coming almost as an extension of the first movement, but one that will reach far greater heights. This fact makes the complete sweep of the symphony apparent, and is certainly a major factor in the unity of the entire work. After the first theme group the movement subsides until a new climax at the closing theme. This is continued well into the development, and from both its length and strength, is the greatest climax yet found. If it were continued too long, no greater climax could be achieved, and the symphony would have to end right here. Instead, at the last possible moment, Beethoven begins a gradual diminishing (bar 195), and the resulting calm before the recapitulation prepares for further climaxes to come. The first theme is abbreviated in the recapitulation and, therefore, its climax is less than that of the beginning of the exposition. Again there is a lull during the second theme, but the climax reached with the return of the closing theme is continued through the entire coda, providing the last and greatest climax of the symphony. The coda does have momentary lulls for reasons of contrast, but it is essentially climactic. Indeed, it reaches even greater heights near the end, as indicated by two places marked *triple forte*, a most unusual dynamic marking for Beethoven. It is as if he is telling the orchestra to play louder than they have ever played in their lives, and to this day orchestras strain to reach a superhuman level of excitement at this point.

This symphony can be seen to be a single composition, although it is large and diverse. Some of this unity is achieved by readily discernible techniques, and some of it by means less tangible, but nevertheless very real. This same is true of any multimovement composition, and an examination and description of the various movements will reveal at least to some degree the over-all design of any such piece.

THE BAROQUE SONATA

Although many works called sonatas were written in the Baroque Era, it is not possible to deal very specifically with their structures, for they exhibit considerable variety. A few general observations can be made, but an intensive study of the history of the period and of its vast literature is necessary to develop an understanding of the various ways in which the term *sonata* was used.

One common type of Baroque sonata consists of four movements in a slow – fast – slow – fast relationship. Since these sonatas predate the development of sonata form, a complex version of binary and sometimes ternary form is often used for individual movements. Sometimes one or both of the slow movements end with a half cadence, depending on the fast movement that follows for harmonic completeness. In this case, the slow and fast movements seem to combine into a single unit that is larger than a movement, a practice that has been noted in the earlier discussion of the sonata. The number of movements in these Baroque sonatas is not always standard, many other patterns being found. The pattern of fast – slow – fast, which we have already seen, is quite common. The number of movements may greatly exceed four or be considerably less than four; sometimes only one movement is found. Notable examples of this last practice are the keyboard sonatas of Domenico Scarlatti.

Baroque sonatas are divided into two distinct types. The *sonata da chiesa* (church sonata) most commonly used the slow – fast – slow – fast pattern already mentioned and tended to be a rather serious work. The *sonata da camera* (chamber sonata) usually consisted of several dance movements and was a lighter work. It is in some ways comparable to the dance suite which will be next discussed.

THE BAROQUE DANCE SUITE

A common type of multimovement composition in the Baroque Era, written both for keyboard solo and for larger mediums such as orchestra, was the dance suite. Since these were never intended for actual dancing, they contain highly stylized versions of several types of dances. In some cases the nature of the music is so altered that little remains to suggest the dance. As in the case of the Baroque sonata, there is considerable variety in the movement plan of the dance suite, and only general observations about the form are possible. However, by the time of Bach the movement plan of the suite was fairly standardized, and it is this plan that will be discussed.

The dance suite of Bach's time consisted of four basic movements, an allemande, a courante, a sarabande, and a gigue. Very often the suite had more movements, one or more other dances being inserted between the sarabande and the gigue. The dances commonly used for this purpose included the minuet, bourrée, gavotte, passepied, polonaise, rigaudon, anglaise, and the loure. In addition, a non-dance movement called an *air* is quite common. The dance movements are sometimes preceded by a prelude, and are usually in a binary or ternary form, the former being far more common. If there is a prelude, it may be in some free form or in ritornello form, a form which will be studied in Chapter VIII.

CYCLIC FORM

In most multimovement works there is no thematic connection between the various movements; that is, each movement has its own set of themes. *Cyclic form* refers to the practice of using a theme in more than one movement, and in the most extreme cases one or more themes will be found in all movements. In spite of its obvious usefulness in achieving unity between the movements of a work, this technique is not very commonly used. In Chapter III the use of a basic motive to connect themes of different movements was discussed, but the term *cyclic form* suggests a more direct connection between themes of movements than this, since in cyclic form the actual melody of one movement is transferred to another movement. Cyclic form is particularly associated with the school of Cèsar Franck, and is a basic principle in the composition of his *Symphony in D Minor*. The *Idée Fixe* used by Berlioz is an earlier example of this same practice, and there are many examples from much earlier times. Occasionally composers who usually made no attempt to use themes in more than one movement tried this technique. Such is the case of the finale of Mozart's *Third Horn Concerto in E Flat, K. 447* which uses the theme of the slow movement transformed to six-eight time as the theme for the middle episode of the rondo finale. Any music that has common themes between movements can be said to be cyclic in nature, although the term is applied particularly to certain works of the late nineteenth century and the twentieth century.

A technique related to cyclic form is the process of theme transformation. If the same theme is to appear in more than one movement, it must conform to the time signature and tempo of each movement, and may have to be drastically altered to do so. One of the weaknesses of cyclic form is that a small number of themes are used for many movements. If these themes are radically altered, a far greater degree of thematic variety results. Also composers find that the alteration of themes has an obvious effect on their meaning, and is therefore a valuable expressive device.

ONE-MOVEMENT FORM

The composer Liszt made use of an interesting variant of sonata form that, while it aroused little interest among other composers in his century, must fascinate contemporary composers, since they make frequent use of it. This form consists of writing a long movement with several contrasting sections which give the effect of each of the movements that would be normally found in a sonata type of piece. Such a work might be in sonata form, starting out with a fast section which is an exposition. The development section that follows would develop material from the exposition, but be in the nature of a slow movement. A second part of the development could be like a scherzo, after which the recapitulation would return the original fast tempo of the exposition, thus creating the effect of a fast finale. Thus the entire work is a single movement in sonata form, yet also gives the effect of four movements—first movement, slow movement, scherzo, and finale. The term for such a piece is *one-movement form*. Two works are discussed here to clarify this form. The Liszt sonata is chosen because it is a pioneer work in this form and the Barber symphony provides a contemporary example.

Liszt: *Piano Sonata in B Minor*

This sonata offers an excellent introduction to one-movement form. The various elements of the form are clearly present, partly because this is a very early example of the technique. Since the entire sonata is based on a total of five themes, the melodic material is very concentrated. The one long movement that constitutes the sonata can be seen in an over-all view to be a sonata form with a short introduction and a long coda. As such it is not unlike the sonata form movements of Beethoven, but the variety of expression within it and its length are a product of the one-movement technique. Since the total design of this sonata is a combination of two different formal plans, sonata form and the plan of a three-movement sonata, the work can best be approached by considering each of these plans separately. The sonata form will be considered first.

The slow introduction presents the first important melody of the sonata, and this will be called the *introduction theme*. The sonata form starts with the first theme which is presented at the *Allergo energico*. This theme contains two more important melodic ideas, part one of the first theme occurring at the beginning of the *Allegro,* and part two in its seventh bar. The first theme is extensive and forceful and is followed by a transition which is based on the introduction theme. This leads to the second theme which is in three-two time and marked *Grandioso*. The key pattern of this exposition is quite regular, the first theme being in the tonic key of B minor, and the second theme in D major, the relative major. There is no closing theme due to the climactic nature of the second theme. The second theme is really quite short and breaks off at a hold. There follows immediately a development of the first theme, and all that follows until the recapitulation is development. This development section will be discussed in more detail in the consideration of the three-movement aspect of the sonata.

The recapitulation comes about two-thirds of the way through the work, and is in the form of a fugue on the first part of the first theme. This fugue is marked *Allegro energico* and is in the key of B flat minor, a half step lower than the key of the exposition. The seven bars preceding the start of the fugue contain the material of the introduction a half step lower than the original introduction. The recapitulation of the slow introduction as well as of the first theme is a common technique in sonata forms of the twentieth century, but rare in the time of Liszt. The fugue subject incorporates both the first and second parts of the first theme. Eventually the head of the subject is heard in inversion. This entire fugato, as it should be called, should be studied in detail after the technique has been discussed in Chapter IX. After the fugal passage, part of the first theme returns in a form very similar to that of the exposition, and the same transition based on the introduction theme is again used. As might be expected, the second theme recapitulates in the tonic key of B major. Again it is short and breaks off with a hold. An extensive coda follows that returns themes from the entire sonata, not as a further recapitulation, but as a final reminiscence before the work ends.

The other approach to the form of this sonata is to consider that we have a complete three-movement sonata with the usual fast – slow – fast movements. From this point of view, the exposition is the first movement, the development is the slow movement, and the recapitulation is the last movement, the coda in this case serving as a coda to the entire sonata and not as a coda to the last movement alone. This view of the sonata is as valid as the sonata-form view, and the ingenuity of the form is that both views are possible, since both functions can be readily seen.

The analysis of the middle movement, or development section, of this sonata starts with the hold that ended the second theme in the exposition. There is immediately a development of the first part of the first theme, but the mood is different, being more gentle. Thus Liszt already hints as the character of the slow movement. About a page after the development starts the second part of the first theme is presented in an augmented version. The mood of this theme is completely altered, and in this new form it functions as the theme of the slow movement. The development of both parts of the first theme continues, always in the character of a slow movement, until a cadenza-like passage interrupts. This serves to indicate a major division of the form, and the section that follows returns the fiery mood of the exposition and is devoted to further development of the first theme. This section ends with a forceful climax, and a recitative divides it from the section to follow. This new recitative is introduced by a forceful statement of the second theme in the minor mode. The third and last section of the development begins in three-four time with the tempo marking *Andante sostenuto*. Here is the slow movement proper, the first section of the development being more a foreshadowing of the slow movement than a part of it. This new section starts with a new theme, the fifth of the five melodies in the sonata. Liszt introduces a new theme in the slow movement to suggest by theme as well as by mood that it is a separate movement. Later in the slow movement this theme is returned to create the suggestion of a ternary form. The other two themes of this slow movement are the second theme and the calm version of the second part of the first theme that was introduced early in the development. This section gradually dies away and flows into the return of the introduction.

An effective feature of this development section is the use of the cadenza-like passages to separate the three sections. Of these three, the middle section is the most like the development, complete with the mood of the exposition. The last section is definitely the slow movement, but the first section is an enigma, since it both introduces the mood and one of the themes of the slow movement, and also serves as a development section. The ambiguity of the function of this section is part of the effectiveness of the form of the sonata.

The coda, which follows the hold that ends the second theme in the recapitulation, presents all the themes of the sonata. The first part of the coda uses the version of the first theme that is found in the slow movement, but eventually all the themes are treated: the introduction theme, both parts of the first theme, the slow movement theme, and the second theme, this last in its most triumphant form. But instead of ending the sonata triumphantly, Liszt ends it with a final statement of the introduction in the original key and mood, so that the form of the sonata is completely rounded. If the form were described without quoting the themes, one might feel that a contemporary piece was being discussed, so advanced is the formal thinking. It is unfortunate that the sentimentality of the music and overworking of the diminished seventh chord sometimes obscures Liszt's considerable talent as the creator of highly original musical forms.

Samuel Barber: *First Symphony, Op. 9*

This work is subtitled to indicate that it is in one movement, and is discussed here to illustrate the contemporary composer's interest in this form. The symphony opens with the conventional exposition of a sonata form, which presents three themes, a first theme starting in the second bar, a second theme two bars before number 2, [2] and

---

[2] The rehearsal numbers are those found in the score published by G. Schirmer, Inc., New York.

a closing theme two bars before number 6. The entire symphony makes extensive use of these themes, and the first of them in particular is subjected to many transformations, some of which will be shown to demonstrate the process of thematic transformation. The original form of the first theme is seen in Example 81.

EXAMPLE 81

As in the case of the twentieth-century examples previously discussed, tempo change is used to delineate the three sections of the exposition: first theme, second theme, and closing theme. This last part extends from two bars after number 4 to number 8. A development begins at 8 with a presentation of the first theme, and proceeds to develop other themes as well. The development reaches a climax at number 12 which, in turn, leads to a final-sounding ending two bars after 15. This is the end of the first large section of the symphony. The *Allegro molto* that follows is a scherzo and uses as its theme the transformation of the first theme of the sonata form shown in Example 82.

EXAMPLE 82

Thus while this is the equivalent of a new movement, development of the sonata form themes continues. The scherzo starts as a fugue, and is well worth a more detailed analysis than is possible here. The scherzo climaxes with a version of the first theme, seen in Example 83, after which it ends very quickly.

Multimovement Compositions   131

EXAMPLE 83

A slow movement follows immediately at the *Andante tranquillo* between 33 and 34. Since this section uses a version of the second theme of the sonata form, the process of development continues. This builds slowly to a climax, and after 41, at the *Con moto*, three-four time, the final section of the symphony begins. This is a passacaglia which uses as its ground bass still another version of the first theme. The ground is six bars long and can be seen with the beginning of its repetition in Example 84.

EXAMPLE 84

One bar after 43 in the strings a form of the closing theme of the exposition appears, so that all three themes are used in either the scherzo, the slow movement, or the passacaglia. These themes are used far more than is shown in this analysis, and this too should be the subject of further study. One other transformation of the first theme is presented in Example 85. This occurs at number 45 in counterpoint with the ground bass form of this theme. The symphony ends with a short coda.

Unlike the Liszt sonata, this symphony has no recapitulation as such. However, as has been said, all the themes return late in the work. Thus there is still the dual relationship of one-movement form. The whole symphony at least suggests a sonata form, although it may be also viewed as a four-movement work: first movement, scherzo, slow movement, and passacaglia.

EXAMPLE 85

EXAMPLES FOR ANALYSIS

Examples of multimovement works are so numerous that there is no need to mention any specific works.

CYCLIC FORM

Franck: *Symphony in D Minor*

Tchaikovsky: *Symphony No. 4 in F Minor, Op. 36*

Tchaikovsky: *Symphony No. 5 in E Minor ,Op. 64*

ONE-MOVEMENT FORM

Harris: *Third Symphony*

Schoenberg: *First Chamber Symphony, Op. 9*

Sibelius: *Symphony No. 7 in C, Op. 105*

VIII

Ritornello

Form and the

Concerto Grosso

MELODY RARELY stands alone in the music of the Western world. Instead it is one part of a musical texture, being accompanied either by a harmonic setting or by other melodies. Even in the latter case a harmonic background is still established. For this reason, an instrument that can play only a single melodic line or a singer is rarely heard alone, but rather is heard either as a part of a larger performing group, or as a soloist with an accompaniment. In music of a more intimate nature, this accompaniment is furnished by a piano or some such instrument, but in a more elaborate piece in a larger concert hall, the accompaniment is furnished by a large group such as an orchestra. The problem of balancing a medium that uses a single singer or instrumentalist accompanied by an orchestra has already been mentioned in Chapter V. At that time it was noted that a solution to this problem might well be achieved through manipulation of the form, and one such form was studied, the classical concerto. This chapter will further explore this problem and composers' solutions to it.

The study of a form such as this provides insight into the interplay between musical form and the other elements of music, such as melody, accompaniment, and performance medium.

RITORNELLO FORM

Although the solution created by the composers of the Baroque Era cannot in any way be compared to the form of the classical concerto, the two forms do share a common origin; that is, both were created to fuse successfully the elements of a medium which are difficult to balance. The Baroque solution to this problem is the ritornello form.[1] The term comes from the instrumental interludes of very early Baroque operas, and since the form has a vocal origin, we will discuss its use in vocal music first.

An aria for solo singer and orchestra using ritornello form starts with a forceful passage for the orchestra alone. This is the ritornello, and it must both have a definite beginning and ending, and be very solidly in the tonic key of the aria. The basic design of the form is based on a tonal arch. From time to time throughout the aria the ritornello returns, each time in a new key, and the work ends with a tonic statement of the ritornello. These recurrent ritornellos serve two functions: they are one basic element in the form of the piece which is the exclusive property of the orchestra, and as such insure its importance, and they furnish pauses in the voice part necessitated by a long aria. Between the ritornellos come the passages for the singer, and these are known as *episodes*.[2] Since each successive ritornello is in a new key, one of the functions of an episode is to modulate from the key of the ritornello that preceded it to the key of the one that will follow. The episode also offers a contrast to the ritornello, since the latter is a passage which is solidly in a single key.

This description of the function of the episodes makes them sound like passages which are considerably less important to the form than the ritornellos. This can hardly be the case, since this form has its origins in vocal music. As has already been seen in Chapter VI, the voice part is always the most important part in

---

[1] There is no widely accepted name for this form, although it is very common in the Baroque Era, and is certainly well understood by anyone considering this music. *Ritornello form* is used because it is suggestive of the origin of the form and because there is some precedent for it in the technical literature.

[2] This term has been also used used for a rather similar passage in rondo form. It is not inappropriate to make the comparison suggested by this double use of this term.

a vocal composition because it is the singer who conveys the words which represent the primary purpose of the piece. Thus the presence of the singer and the text emphasizes the episodes, and the importance of the orchestral ritornellos to the form insures the balance between the two halves of the medium. In practice additional emphasis is often given to the episodes by making them longer than the ritornellos.

J. S. Bach: *Mass in B Minor, No. 10—Quoniam Tu Solus Sanctus*

This aria for bass has an obbligato part for solo French horn, a common practice in the Baroque Era and one that is not restricted to ritornello form. For this reason, this analysis will not treat the use of the horn, other than to note that it dominates all the ritornellos.

The aria starts with a ritornello which is very solidly in the tonic key of D major. The singer enters in bar 13 with a slightly different version of the melody of the ritornello. At bar 20 the horn has the beginning of the ritornello melody and at bar 33 this same figure is in the vocal line. Finally, at bar 45, the singer cadences in the dominant key of A major and the second ritornello follows in that key. It is a very common practice to abridge one or more of the ritornellos, and this new one is four bars shorter than the first. As is the case with the rondo theme in rondo form, this abridgement avoids having too many literal repetitions of the same material. Also, the ritornello is more familiar each time it is heard and need not be as long to make the listener aware of it.

The second episode, from bar 53 to bar 67, starts in A major and ends in B minor. Although all the episodes use the same basic melodic material, no two are alike, for it is here that the composer has the most freedom within the form. This is to be expected since it is the episodes that set the text, and if the form of the episodes were too restricted it would be impossible to accommodate all texts. The third ritornello, which follows directly in bar 67, is in the relative minor key, B minor. It is the same length as the second ritornello, but is not the same abridgement, for this ritornello is essentially the last two-thirds of the first ritornello.

The third episode starts in bar 75 with the same melodic material that started the second episode, but moves on to a new treatment of the same material. In bar 90 the opening of the first episode is found, almost creating the impression of a recapitulation. As will be seen in the discussion of the fugue, the last episode often returns material from the opening episode. Since this brings the chorus that follows, an interesting way to connect two move-back the very first entrance of the singer, a fairly rounded form results. In this case bars 90 to 98 are essentially the same as bars 13 to 21, after which the episode comes rather quickly to a close. At bar 116 the last ritornello begins in the tonic key. It is identical to the first ritornello except that its last chord is the first chord of ments. While it is common to abridge many of the middle ritornellos, the last ritornello is usually identical with the first one, so that the movement ends exactly as it started.

The basic key pattern of the work just studied is the key pattern of the ritornellos: tonic – dominant – relative – tonic. This is a common key pattern for ritornello form, and is similar to the tonal structure found in many other forms that we have studied. If there is a ritornello in the subdominant key, it will come late in the movement—the common treatment of this key. The key pattern of a ritornello form may be as extensive as a composer wishes it to be, but each successive ritornello will be in a new key, with the exception of the last which will of course be tonic. Since the basic tonal design of a ritornello form is a tonal arch, the movement must have at least three ritornellos and two episodes so that the middle ritornello can present a contrasting key, nearly always the dominant.

A good example of this minimum size of ritornello form is the *Agnus Dei* from this same composition. No doubt the slow tempo influenced Bach to use this brief design of the form. The first ritornello is in G minor, the second in D minor, and the third returns to G minor. The second and third ritornellos are half as long as the first one.

The Messiah of Handel has many movements in ritornello form, and for this reason a movement of this work is discussed next. This movement is basically a solo for the alto. Although the chorus participates late in the movement, it has no effect on the basic structure of the form.

Handel: *The Messiah, No. 9—O Thou That Tellest Good Tidings to Zion*

The movement starts with a twelve-bar ritornello in the tonic key of D major. The singer enters with the melody of the ritornello, and throughout the work the episodes make considerable use of the melodic material of the ritornello. The first episode ends in bar 35 in the key of the dominant, A major. Bars 36 through 40 are the second ritornello in the dominant key. This ritornello consists basically of the middle third of the first ritornello with a forceful ending to close securely in the key of A major. The second episode starts in bar 41, but instead of starting in the key of A major, the key of the second ritornello, it starts in the tonic key of D. Furthermore, the singer starts this new episode with the very same melodic line that was found at the beginning of the first episode, so that the two episodes are more than usually related. The episode proceeds to use the thematic material in new ways, and comes to an end in bar 67 in the key of G major, the subdominant.

The third ritornello starts at once in this key, and here too the full length of the first ritornello is not used. This time the last third of the first ritornello is used, so that a different portion of the whole ritornello is used each time. This is a common means of abridging the ritornello, since it assures equal treatment of the material in the first ritornello in successive ritornellos. The third episode, which follows in bar 72, starts exactly the same as the first two episodes, in the tonic key of D major. This technique further reinforces the parallel nature of the three episodes and also puts greater emphasis on the tonic key than is usual with this form. This last episode is extended by the entrance of the chorus. Each section of the chorus enters with the basic theme of the movement that was first presented at the beginning of the first ritornello, and was also used to start each episode. After a rather climactic choral passage, the movement ends with the final ritornello in the tonic key of D major. This time the ritornello is complete and is exactly as it was first heard.

Because of the nature of the expression of this movement, Handel did not choose to use the key of the relative minor, but beyond this the key pattern of the ritornellos is typical. The inclusion of a passage for chorus suggests that this form is suitable for choral use as well as for solo arias. The next work discussed illustrates the ritornello form used for an elaborate choral movement.

J. S. Bach: *Mass in B Minor, No. 17—Et Resurrexit*

It is necessary to consider the preceding movement, the *Crucifixus*, to come to a full understanding of the form of this movement. The *Crucifixus* is a very somber set of variations over a ground bass, the mood fitting the nature of the subject, while the next movement, which describes the resurrection of Christ, is in a completely different mood. The *Crucifixus* is in the key of E minor, but ends on a G major chord which gives no sense of finality. The next movement starts at once on the text *Et resurrexit* (He has risen) in the key of D major. The literature has few passages which exceed this moment in dramatic intensity, and to achieve such a peak of excitement, the chorus must enter at once with the words, the convention that the orchestra alone starts a ritornello form notwithstanding.

The first ritornello occupies eight bars, cadencing in the ninth bar in the tonic key of D major. It is a completely normal ritornello except for the presence of the chorus in the first three bars. The first episode starts with imitative entrances of a melody which is derived from the beginning of the ritornello but is independently identifiable because of a long sixteenth-note run. The imitative entrances build quickly to a climax which is heightened by the high B in the soprano part in bar 15. The first episode is long in relation to the nine-bar ritornello, extending to bar 34 for a total length of twenty-five bars. By this time it has modulated to the dominant key, and the second ritornello follows in the key of A major. This new ritornello is sixteen bars long, nearly twice as long as the first one. It is unusual for the second ritornello to be longer, but here again the text and expression of the piece furnish an explanation. Just as the chorus was used at the beginning to present the text at once, so the first ritornello was as short as possible so that the chorus could continue with the text. By the second ritornello there is no longer the pressing need for the words to be ever-present, and therefore Bach can write a ritornello which is more in proportion to the size of the episodes.

The second episode starts in bar 50 in the key of A major, and continues to bar 66. A brief instrumental interlude occurs in bars 56 and 57. This is not a ritornello, but rather a short interlude within an episode, since it is not nearly as long as a ritornello. Brief passages such as this one are found in both vocal and instrumental ritornello forms, but no confusion occurs in the labeling if the relative sizes of these interludes and the ritornellos are considered. The third ritornello starts in bar 66 and is in the relative minor key, B minor. This ritornello is no longer than the first ritornello and ends in bar 74.

The last episode is long, extending from bar 75 to bar 107. It consists of two sections, the first containing the long passage for the bass section alone and the subsequent choral climax (bars 75 to 88). The second section begins at bar 92 and continues to the end of the episode. This section starts with imitative entrances of the theme that began the first episode and are even preceded by a short orchestral interlude that is reminiscent of the first ritornello. Here is another example of the return in the last episode of a portion of the first episode. The last ritornello is the longest, occupying the twenty bars from bar 108 to the end. It is in the tonic key of D major, and again its length may be explained by the fact that the first ritornello was unusually short.

This work suggests two further complications that will be found in many ritornello forms. One of these is the existence of a new theme, or a distinct version of an old theme, which is used exclusively in the episodes. The other is the intermixing of the two elements of the medium in both areas of the form, so that the chorus or soloist may be present during brief moments of the ritornello, and conversely, may be missing briefly in the episodes. If all other aspects of the form are normal, this need cause no problem in analysis, but care must be taken to avoid being too dependent on the use of the medium to distinguish ritornellos from episodes.

THE CONCERTO GROSSO

The concerto grosso is a creation of the Baroque Era, and most examples of it come from that period. The Classic Era which followed preferred the variant of sonata form for the concerto. This form replaced the Baroque concerto technique, although there has been a revival of the concerto grosso in this century which will be dealt with later. A definition of *concerto grosso* is more concerned with the performance medium and its use than with the forms involved. The concerto grosso is a type of concerto in which there is a small solo instrumental group rather than the usual single soloist. This group is called the *concertino* and most often consists of two violins and continuo (cello plus keyboard instrument). The solo group is self-sufficient, since it consists of several instruments of different ranges as well as a keyboard instrument to play the harmonic background. Thus it is possible for the solo group to play passages by themselves, with no need of the accompaniment of the orchestra, a fact which has direct bearing on the use of the medium. Furthermore, since orchestras of the Baroque Era were very small by present-day standards, the accompanying orchestra could not achieve a very great climax unless the solo group was added to it. This leads to the concept of the *tutti*, which, as its name suggests, is a passage in which all the instruments play, soloists and orchestra alike. The accompanying orchestra is sometimes known as the *ripieno*, although this term is sometimes also used as synonymous with tutti, and is therefore difficult to define properly.[3] All this suggests that the medium of the concerto grosso consists of three elements, the group of soloists, the accompanying orchestra, and a third force consisting of the first two groups used together. In practice this is usually not the case; the orchestra is rarely used alone for any major section of the form. The basic contrast is between the soloists, either used alone or accompanied by the orchestra, and the tutti passages.

The two uses of the medium fit very well the requirements of ritornello form. The tutti passages are the ritornellos, and the passages that feature the soloists are the episodes. This is a basic change in the use of the medium as compared with vocal ritornello forms, in which the entire medium is actually used in the episodes but not in the ritornellos. This is no reversal of the nature of the form, however, since in an aria the orchestral passages may well be full and climactic while the vocal passages are severely limited in the fullness of sound possible if the singer is to be heard. From this point of view, the ritornellos are full passages and the episodes are more thinly scored, a fact that adds to the importance of the ritornellos.

For this reason, and also because a group of solo instruments has nothing that compares in importance to the text in vocal music, the concerto use of this form is in danger of putting too great an emphasis on the ritornellos. The standard solution to this problem is the same as that found in the classical concerto; a thematic distinction is made between the two sections of the form. In a concerto grosso it is common for the solo instruments to introduce a new theme at the beginning of the first episode. While the episodes may in part be devoted to development of themes from the ritornellos, the soloists' theme is found only in the episodes, and is the exclusive property of the soloists. This inequality in the treatment of the themes seems sufficient to restore the balance of the form and to

[3] A typical use of the term *ripieno* occurs in the *Fifth Brandenburg Concerto of* Bach, where the solo violin part in the concertino is labeled *Violino principale,* and the violin section in the orchestra is labeled *Violino di ripieno.*

keep ritornello and episode equal in importance. This seems a logical explanation of the fact that while many instrumental ritornello forms have a new theme in the first episode, vocal uses of the form rarely do, the singer instead drawing on the themes of the ritornello for all thematic material.

The six *Brandenburg Concertos* of Bach offer examples of large and complex instrumental ritornello forms. In these concertos the general outline of the form is the same as that previously studied, but some details of the structure are freer, and the simple concept of the form previously described is of only limited usefulness. For this reason we will examine a movement of one of these concertos, both to see a concerto grosso that uses this form, and also to consider a more extended example of it. Another unusual feature of these concertos is that none of them uses the usual two violins and continuo as the concertino group. The concerto that we are to study uses the most unusual concertino of the six, a fact that has a very profound effect on its form.

J. S. Bach: *Brandenburg Concerto No. 2 in F—1st Movement*

The concertino for this concerto consists of a flute, an oboe, a violin, and a trumpet. The trumpet is written in the extremely high register commonly used in the Baroque Era for melodic trumpet parts. Since valves had not yet been invented, only in this register could the scale notes be produced, and these were desired if the instrument were to play a melodic part. When this work is played today it is apparent that the trumpet part is by far the most difficult of the four solo parts, and that although the soloists are theoretically equal the most important of the soloists is the trumpet. Surely this trumpet part was no easier in Bach's day, and this inequality of the soloists must also have existed when the work was written. This is apparent even from the role of the trumpet in the form of the piece, and is an interesting example of the modification of a form due to the special nature of the medium. Generations of study of Bach's music as counterpoint specimens have tended to create the impression that he was a composer who wrote very fine counterpoint that somehow existed independently of the performance medium, and to obscure Bach's great skill at utilizing the medium of a piece, often in a very colorful way. It is hoped that the study of this concerto, and especially of the treatment of the trumpet, will serve to illustrate Bach's great sensitivity to the performance medium.

The movement opens with an eight-bar tutti ritornello. The theme of the ritornello has three distinct ideas that are important to the form and will be identified as the three parts of the ritornello theme: part one starting in the first measure, part two in bar 3, and part three in bar 5. Also of interest is the bass line that accompanies the first part of the ritornello theme. The parts of the ritornello melody are important since they will be developed separately in the episodes, and also since any combination of them may be used for future ritornellos. Following the first ritornello, the soloists are introduced one at a time. The soloists enter playing a new theme, the theme belonging exclusively to the soloists and the episodes. The passages that introduce each soloist are not all episode; rather fragments of the ritornello are heard between each solo entrance. The violin enters first, followed in order by oboe, flute, and trumpet, thus saving until last the climactic trumpet entrance. The tutti interlude between the violin and oboe entrance is in the tonic key of F, but the next two tutti passages, at bars 15 and 19, are in the dominant key of C major. These last two tuttis offer the most striking instance of the effect of the trumpet on the form of the work. The bass melody that accompanied the first part of the ritornello theme has already been mentioned, and in the tuttis under discussion, an inversion takes place. The first part of the ritornello theme remains in a similar position in the first violin part, and the bass line moves above it into the solo trumpet part. Thus the trumpet plays a spectacular part in the presentation of a passage in invertible counterpoint even before its formal introduction on the soloists' theme in bar 21. Since no other solo instrument, not even the other three together, could perform this task, it is evident that the special ability of the trumpet played a basic part in the planning of this concerto. After the formal trumpet entrance in bar 21, the ritornello in C major is completed, cadencing in bar 28.

In bar 29 the trumpet plays the soloists' theme a second time, now in the key of F. This not only gives this theme to the trumpet twice, but since this second time it is a fourth higher than it was at first, it puts the trumpet unbelievably high. At bar 31 a new ritornello starts in D minor, the relative minor. This is really a new form of the ritornello, one that starts in an almost tentative way. It contains the figure of three eighth notes and a half note seen first in the trumpet in bars 32 and 33, and the suspensions in the first and second violins seen in bars 33, 34, and 35. This form of the ritornello will be used three times in the movement, always in the minor mode, and it must be thought of as a variant of the ritornello for this mode. This D minor ritornello ends in bar 39 and a long episode follows. It is devoted to development of fragments from the ritornello, and in bar 46 it comes close to suggesting a ritornello in the tonic key.

The next actual ritornello begins in bar 56 in the subdominant key of B flat. It consists of only the third part of the ritornello theme, thus following the practice of abridging a ritornello in the middle of the piece. This subdominant ritornello occurs at the center of the movement, and creates a suggestion of the movement starting anew. This impression is strengthened by the soloists entering on their theme in bar 60, just as they did at the start of the first episode, although this time they follow one another directly. The order of entrance is changed so that the flute enters first in B flat major, the violin next in G minor, the oboe third in E flat major, and the trumpet last in C minor. Notice that each successive key is a third lower, and also that while the order is changed the climactic trumpet is still saved for last. This episode continues until the fifth ritornello starts in bar 75. This new ritornello is in the key of G minor, the supertonic key and also the relative minor of B flat, the key of the previous ritornello. Again we have the minor form of the ritornello, which lasts until the middle of bar 83. An episode developing fragments from the ritornello follows, continuing until bar 94 where a sixth ritornello in A minor is found. This, too, is the version of the ritornello used in minor and ends in bar 102.

This movement has an unusual tonal arch in that, instead of moving slowly away from the tonic key and then gradually returning, the tonality has been moving further and further from F major until the last ritornello has ended with a cadence in A minor, the mediant key of F, and one that is very remote. Instead of following this cadence with an episode, Bach immediately introduces the last ritornello in the tonic key in bar 103. There is no modulation as such; rather the piece stops in the key of A minor and starts at once in F, a very dramatic way to return to the tonic key. The drama of the beginning of the last ritornello is heightened by having both the soloists and the orchestra play the first part of the ritornello theme in octaves, even the keyboard player being directed to play only the melody. Evidently because this last ritornello is the only section in the tonic key at the end of the piece, Bach found it desirable to extend it by inserting several quiet bars that feature the soloists, beginning in bar 107. After this momentary lull, the ritornello continues and ends exactly as the first ritornello ended, thus emphasizing the relation between the two.

While the other two movements of this concerto are not in ritornello form, further consideration must be given to the use of the trumpet in these movements. After the first movement, with its extreme range, including three sounding high G's, the most practical use for the trumpet in the slow movement is to let the player rest, and this is just what Bach does. It might also be noted that the forceful nature of the trumpet in its highest register is not particularly well suited to a slow singing movement. The finale is a fugue, and the first entrance of the fugue subject is in the trumpet. As in the case of the first movement, the trumpet dominates the finale, and the concerto ends with the fugue subject in the trumpet, thus continuing the prominence of this instrument to the end.

The ritornello form was also used by composers of the Baroque Era to write concertos for a single solo instrument. Such works made very similar use of the form, and there is no need to consider a work of this type separately. The form was also of use in the composition of sonatas, but is found only in those in which the keyboard part is written out, since if the keyboard part is written as figured bass, the melodic content of the ritornello is not sufficiently under the composer's control. In a sonata for violin or flute and keyboard instrument, the keyboard instrument may play the ritornellos by itself, but since this makes the medium of the ritornellos thin both instruments are often used in both the ritornellos and the episodes. In this case, although there is usually no problem in identifying the parts of the form, the use of the medium is obviously of little assistance.

Not every concerto grosso makes use of ritornello form. Alternation of texture is a very basic element of the Baroque concerto, and one that is not restricted to works that use ritornello form, for this treatment of solo and tutti is also characteristic of the next work discussed. In this piece the texture shifts more frequently, since the forms used do not demand the comparatively long sections in one texture characteristic of ritornello form.

Corelli: *Concerto VIII, Op. 6, No. 8 (Fatto per Notte di Natale—* Christmas Concerto)

This concerto contains a bewildering number of movements, many of which are short and fragmentary. As has been seen earlier, when there are a number of short movements in a work, they tend to combine to suggest a smaller number of movements which contain several moods within them. In the present work it is difficult to say just what should be called a movement, and the grouping of movements which will be discussed here is at least in part subjective. There seem to be six separately identifiable movements, a large number. With so many movements some will be short, and since these may well be through-composed, it is difficult to say much about the general nature of the forms of all the movements. The first movement consists of two sections, a brief *Vivace*, and a somewhat longer *Grave*. Taken together both sections serve little more than as an introduction to the second movement, which is marked *Allegro*. This is a more important movement, not only because it is much longer, but because it is in a binary form, the use of an organized and rounded form giving it greater scope.

The first two movements are in the tonic key of G minor, but the third movement is in a contrasting key, E flat major. The parts of the ternary form of the third movement contrast greatly, and there is little unity of mood within the movement. The first and third sections, both *Adagio*, are alike except for an extension of the last part to end the movement. The middle section, marked *Allegro*, is very agitated. The fourth movement is a short *Vivace* in binary form in the tonic key of G minor, also the key of the next movement. The fifth movement is a ternary form, as if Corelli wished to alternate the use of binary and ternary form. This time the first and third sections of the form are not identical, and the whole movement consists of two repeated strains, a technique that we have found before in ternary form. This fifth movement, which is an *Allegro*, passes without pause to the final movement which is the *Pastorale* that gives the concerto its name. The key changes to G major for this movement, which is also a ternary form.

The *Brandenburg Concerto* discussed earlier and Corelli's concerto illustrate the two basic formal practices in concerto grosso. Either there are three movements in the basic fast – slow – fast pattern, or there are a number of movements, many quite short, in simple forms. To a great extent these observations also apply to the various kinds of sonatas written in the Baroque Era.

The Classic and Romantic Eras produced several important concertos for two or more soloists, but these are not properly called concerti grossi, since they use sonata form and are in every other way like the solo concertos of these periods. Also, the larger orchestra of the late eighteenth and nineteenth centuries made it difficult to achieve the solo–tutti alternation characteristic of the Baroque concerto, since if the soloist were to play with the orchestra in a tutti, he would be swallowed up by the mass of sound.

The twentieth century has turned to earlier eras, notably the Baroque, for inspiration, and as could be expected there is a revival of interest in the concerto grosso. A chamber orchestra or some such small group is used to duplicate the weight of the orchestra in the Baroque Era, and very often aspects of the Baroque style are used as well. In spite of this fact, there is as yet no widespread revival of interest in the ritornello form, and it remains almost completely a product of the Baroque Era. Although many forms that have been studied span a number of historical periods, some others, including ritornello, seem to belong so completely to the era of their origin that they are of little use outside of it.

EXAMPLES FOR ANALYSIS

A logical starting place for the study of ritornello form is the first movement of any of the other *Brandenburg Concertos* of Bach. For this form in a solo concerto and in the music of another composer, the first movement of Vivaldi's *Violin Concerto in A* (Pisendel Concerto), is a clear example. The *Second Flute Sonata in E Flat* of Bach has a first movement that is not only a clear example of this form in a sonata, but also uses the keyboard instrument alone for the ritornellos and has a new theme for the flute in the episodes. Not all examples of this form in sonatas are as clear.

There are many examples of this form in vocal music. Below are listed a few more from the two vocal works used as sources in the chapter.

Handel: *The Messiah*
   No. 3—*Every Valley Shall Be Exalted*
   No. 11—*The People That Walked in Darkness*
   No. 18—*Rejoice Greatly, O Daughter of Zion*

J.S. Bach: *Mass in B Minor*
   No. 9—*Qui Sedes ad Dexteram*
   No. 14—*Et in Unum Dominum*
   No. 18—*Et in Spiritum Sanctum*

IX

Fugue

FUGUE IS more a procedure than a form, and to discuss or describe fugue as a form it is necessary to limit the discussion historically. However, all compositions of the fugal type do have certain characteristics, techniques, and procedures which justify grouping so many diverse pieces under the general heading of fugue. Before consideration of fugue as a form, a few of its basic elements should be defined.[1]

Subject: A fugue is based on a single important theme called a *subject*. The fugue starts with a presentation of the subject without accompaniment, and throughout the fugue it is frequently present.

Countersubject: A theme which is used consistently in counterpoint with the subject is known as a *countersubject*. Since the subject and countersubject may be used in any voice, they must be in

---

[1] Both the nature of the form and the large variety of examples of it make fugue one of the most complex forms to study. It is beyond the scope of an introductory text such as this to treat this form exhaustively, for to do so would require an entire book.

invertible counterpoint. A fugue may have two countersubjects, in which case these and the subject must be in triple counterpoint.

Exposition: A fugue is a strict polyphonic composition written for a specific number of parts or voices. At the beginning of a fugue, each of the voices enters in turn with the subject and then continues to the countersubject, if one is used. This initial section, which is devoted to the presentation of the subject and countersubject, is called an *exposition*. Later sections of the fugue which are also devoted to presenting the subject in its entirety are also called expositions, each new one being numbered to identify it. The first exposition always continues until all the voices have entered, but successive expositions often contain only one appearance of the subject. However, to be considered an exposition, a section must contain the subject in its entirety, not just fragments of it.

Codetta: An exposition sometimes contains a short passage which does not contain the subject, for reasons that will be seen later. This is called a *codetta*. A codetta is usually shorter than the fugue subject and is most often found in the first exposition.

Answer: If an exposition has more than one entrance of the fugue subject, the first entrance will be in the tonic key of the exposition, but the second entrance will be in another key, usually the dominant. This second entrance is then called an *answer*. It is common to continue these names throughout the exposition, calling the appearances of the fugue subject in the tonic key *subject* and the appearances of the fugue subject in the dominant key *answer*. The term *answer* does not mean a new melody, but rather the fugue subject transposed to a second or answering key.

Development: Between the expositions are passages that introduce no new material but rather develop motives and fragments from the first exposition. These passages are called *developments* [2] and are also numbered in succession.

The general plan of the fugue is an alternation of expositions and developments, starting and ending with an an exposition. The first and last expositions are in the tonic key and the intervening expositions are in other keys, making a tonal arch. The developments, which come between the expositions, accomplish the modulation from key to key, sometimes passing through other keys in the proc-

---

[2] The traditional name for these passages is *episode*, but because these passages in a fugue are developmental in nature and because they are dissimilar to sections in other forms called episodes, this alternative term is suggested as being more descriptive.

ess. The form of the fugue has an obvious relationship to the ritornello form, the expositions being the equivalent of the ritornellos
and the developments the equivalent of the episodes.

The fugues of J. S. Bach offer the ideal starting point in the
study of fugue. Bach's output came at the close of the Baroque Era
which saw the development of the fugue, and his fugues offer a sum-
mary of fugal technique to that time. Bach's fugues have, by the
greatness of their music, made such an impression on musicians that
it is impossible even today to compose a fugue without considering
Bach's concept of this form. The best introduction to this concept is
offered by the 48 fugues of the *Well-tempered Clavier*. Even within
such a limited sample of the fugal literature there exists an almost
overwhelming variety of form, so that while the following two
analyses offer an introduction to the form of fugue, it should be
borne in mind that these illustrations must be taken as only general
examples.

J. S. Bach: *Well–tempered Clavier, Vol. I—Fugue No. 2 in C Minor*

This fugue is written for three voices, and except at the very end,
adheres strictly to this number of parts. Although this is a fugue for
a keyboard instrument, it is conventional to use the vocal names for
the parts—in this case soprano, alto, and bass. As is customary, this
fugue starts with a single voice (the alto) stating the subject, after
which each of the other voices enters with the subject. The complete
subject of this fugue is shown in Example 86. Note that the alto does
not stop with the last note of the subject, but rather continues to
move so that the flow of the alto line, and hence of the piece, is unbroken. Since this is a common technique, it is often necessary to
compare several entries of the subject to discover its exact length.

EXAMPLE 86

In the interest of tonal variety in the first exposition, the first
and third voices enter in the tonic key while the second voice enters
in the key of G minor, the dominant key. This is done not to
confound the listener as to what the tonic key is, but rather to
strengthen the feeling of tonic by presenting a closely related sup-

porting key. This modulation within the exposition causes problems for the composer which can be illustrated by the fugue at hand. Since the subject starts and ends with a tonic chord, the first beat of bar 3 brings the C minor chord ending the subject in the alto into harmonic conflict with the G minor tonic chord implied by the answer in the soprano. If the answer were a literal transposition of the subject, it would be written as in Example 87. To avoid this harmonic and tonal conflict Bach altered the third note of the answer from a D to a C. This puts both voices in the beginning of this bar in the key of C minor and postpones the modulation to G minor until the end of the bar.

EXAMPLE 87

Any such alteration of even a single note of the subject creates what is known as a *tonal answer*. If the answer is a literal transposition of the subject, it is said to be a *real answer*. The tonal answer is the usual means of effecting a smooth connection between the two keys found at this point in the fugue. Although the answer in this fugue is altered so that it begins in the key of C minor, its strong cadence at the end firmly establishes its tonic key as G minor. This illustrates that the most important moment tonally in a fugue subject is the strong final cadence. If the bass were to enter in C minor in the beginning of bar 5, a similar conflict of keys would result. The common solution to this problem of returning from the answer key to the subject key is to delay the next entry and write a free passage, the codetta, which accomplishes this modulation. In this fugue, the two-bar codetta uses fragments of the subject and countersubject as its melodic material. The return to the tonic key is the prime function of codettas, but it should be noted that many codettas are shorter than the fugue subject and so serve to break up the monotonous effect of regularly spaced entrances. With the third entrance of the subject in the bass, the first countersubject is found in the soprano and a second countersubject is introduced in the alto. It is customary for each countersubject to be introduced by the voice that introduced the subject and to follow the subject in the other voices.

The first exposition ends with the C minor cadence at the beginning of bar 9. The first development, which starts in the same bar, is based on an imitation of the head of the subject in the soprano and alto over a scale line in the bass derived from the beginning of the first countersubject. The second exposition begins in bar 11 with the subject in the soprano, the first countersubject in the bass, and the second countersubject in the alto. The key is E flat major, the relative key, and the one almost invariably found in the second exposition. This is because while a closely related key is desired, dominant has already been used in the first exposition, and the other closely related key, subdominant, is considered unsuitable so early in a composition. An additional advantage of using the relative key is that the subject and countersubjects are varied by being presented in the opposite mode. Bars 13 and 14 are the second development, the soprano being derived from an inversion of the head of the first countersubject and the alto and bass using the three eighth notes found in both countersubjects. The third exposition starts in bar 15 in G minor, the dominant. The subject is now in the alto, the first countersubject is in the soprano, and the second countersubject in the bass. Note that by this point the subject and both countersubjects have appeared in the bass voice, demonstrating the necessity of their being in triple counterpoint.

The third development, which starts in bar 17, is very ingeniously constructed. The first bar and a half consists of an inversion at the twelfth of the codetta of the first exposition, the original soprano part now being in the bass voice while the alto plays the original alto part and the soprano adds a free part to enrich the harmony. The last half of bar 18 and bar 19 then reinvert the previous bar and a half, but inverting at the octave rather than at the twelfth. Thus the original order of melodies is restored, while the intervals between the parts are changed. Obviously this was planned at the time the codetta was first composed. Exposition Four in bar 20 brings the return of the tonic key. Development Four which follows in bar 22 is closely related to the first development and should be compared to it. Bach is very fond of returning the material of the first development rather literally in the last, thus recapitulating more than just the first exposition at the end of the work. The fifth and final exposition, in the tonic key, starts in the middle of bar 26 with the subject in the bass, the most climactic position for the subject. An interesting substitution of chord is found in the first beat of bar 27 which seems also to have been saved for this spot to make the last exposition the strongest and most effective. The cadence that ends this exposition is extended and leads directly to the coda, which is the last two and half bars. Here we find the subject once more but without the countersubjects and with the last note altered to an E natural to make the last chord the characteristic major tonic. Thus the subject makes a full cycle in this piece, opening the fugue and reappearing one more time in the coda, bringing the fugue to a close on its last note.

J. S. Bach: *Well–tempered Clavier, Vol. I—Fugue No. 21 in B Flat*

This fugue, too, offers a good introduction to the normal design of Bach's fugues. The subject of this fugue is four bars and one note long, and again ends on the characteristic third degree of the scale. An examination of the real answer in Example 88 will show that it is clearly a harmonic impossibility, and again a tonal answer is used to effect the modulation to the dominant key. In this case the first and third notes of the subject are lowered a second.

EXAMPLE 88

The end of the second entry cadences in F and, since this chord can be used as a dominant of the key of B flat to harmonize the beginning of the subject in the bass in bar 9, no codetta is necessary to modulate back to tonic. The rhythm of the first countersubject complements that of the subject, moving more in the first bar than the second. At the same time, the melody of this countersubject is such a good one that it gives no indication that it was composed primarily for use with this subject. This same is true of the second countersubject, which is found in the soprano in bars 9 to 12. The subject and both countersubjects should be examined as melodies by playing the soprano part for the first twelve bars. What is heard is a single long melody which is very appealing, although it consists of the subject and both countersubjects. In bars 9 to 12 where these melodies are heard as triple counterpoint, the very fine rhythmic interrelation of these three melodies is demonstrated. Whether heard as triple counterpoint or as one long melodic line, the subject and countersubjects seem equally impressive.

By the beginning of bar 13 all three voices have entered, the first exposition is complete, and the first development should start. Instead there is an extra entry of the subject in the soprano with the two countersubjects following through in the lower voices. Since the fourth entry is an answer, it is exactly like the fourth entrance in a four-voice fugue, except that the texture remains three parts. This extra entry, which creates the illusion of a fugue of one more voice, is called a *redundant entry*. A redundant entry occurs in the voice that first started the fugue so as not to disturb the passing of the countersubjects through the other voices, and is either a subject or an answer, whichever would normally come next. This example of redundant entry is very clear, but some are not so apparent, since sometimes a redundant entry is found in the first development midway between the first and second expositions. This may still be considered a redundant entry, and therefore a final section of the first exposition, if it has the proper key and subject or answer relationship with the first exposition.

Bars 17 and 18, which begin the first development, reiterate the material of the last two bars of the exposition distributed differently in the voices, and this development then moves to the developmental ideas that dominate the rest of the fugue. The sixteenth notes in the soprano in bars 19, 20, and 21, are derived from the end of the subject, and the bass in the same bars is a free inversion of the head of the subject, although it should also be compared to the second bar of the first countersubject. The second exposition (in G minor, the relative) starts in bar 22 with the subject in the alto against both countersubjects. A second entrance of the subject occurs in bar 26 in the bass. This is in the form of a tonal answer but is in C minor, the subdominant key of G minor, not in the dominant key. Again both countersubjects are present. The second development, which starts in bar 30, is much longer than the first. It is based entirely on the material used in the first development, and the inverted head of the subject is doubled in thirds from bar 33 on. There is a false start of an exposition in bar 35, curiously distorted to start in C minor and to modulate in two bars to E flat major (relative of C minor) so that the final exposition can start in that key in bar 37. This exposition also has two entrances of the subject in a subject-answer relationship and both countersubjects. The initial key is the subdominant but when this key is answered by its dominant, the tonic key of the fugue results, making a further tonic exposition unnecessary. All that remains is a four-bar coda which starts by reiterating the last two bars of the subject and countersubjects, as was done at the end of the first exposition, and then gradually slows to the end.

One further point reveals how completely Bach equated the three voices in importance. The subject occurs three times in the soprano, three times in the alto, and twice in the bass; the first countersubject occurs three times in the soprano, three times in the alto, and once in the bass; and the second countersubject occurs twice in the soprano, once in the alto, and three times in the bass. Thus the subject and each countersubject come at least once in each voice. Example 89 shows a diagram of the entrances of the subject and countersubjects in this fugue and should be studied since it shows clearly how the countersubjects follow the subject through the parts.

EXAMPLE 89: Subject and Countersubject Entrances from Bach: *Well-tempered Clavier, Vol. I—Fugue 21 in B Flat*

	Exposition I				Exposition II		Exposition III	
Soprano	S	CS I	CS II	S	CS I	CS II	S	CS I
Alto		S	CS I	CS II	S	CS I	CS I	S
Bass			S	CS I	CS II	S	CS II	CS II

These two fugues offer a clear but brief introduction to the form of a fugue. It is impossible to study the many forms found in pieces that are essentially fugal in nature, but to give an introduction to some further aspects of this form the most common procedures of fugal construction will be discussed.

SUBJECT AND COUNTERSUBJECT

Since a basic element of fugue is the imitative treatment of the subject, this melody must have an arresting beginning to call attention to itself, even when it is in an inner voice. A subject must also have a varied but solid harmonic basis that clearly establishes its key, since progression of the subject through a series of keys constitutes a major component of the design of a fugue. This strong sense of tonality is usually accomplished by having the subject end with a strong cadence. A fugue subject also needs one or more strong motives that can be developed. Finally, it must be a powerful and engaging melody which will continue to be expressive even after the numerous repetitions required in the course of the fugue.

To a lesser extent these observations are also true of counter-subjects; however, the countersubject cannot overshadow the subject of a fugue. The countersubject and subject are often complementary, the countersubject supplying chord tones to clarify the harmony and rhythmic motion where the subject is static. *WTC–I–12* [3] has a rhyth-mically static subject and two countersubjects which combine to make a continuous flow of sixteenth notes. The subjects and coun-tersubjects of many of the fugues of the *Well–tempered Clavier* should be studied in great detail, as they offer a better demonstra-tion of this element than a lengthy discussion.

THE EXPOSITION SECTIONS

In the first expositions of the two fugues just discussed the even-numbered entrances are answers in the dominant key and thus, in a sense, a fifth higher than the tonic subject. Such a fugue is known as a "fugue in fifths." Other keys may be used for the answer, even in the first exposition, but these are found more rarely, and some like subdominant, occur most frequently early in the history of the form. Bach used an answer in the subdominant key in the fugue from his *Sonata in G Minor* for unaccompanied violin. Contempo-rary composers often use more distantly related keys for entrances in the exposition and may even have only the first entrance in the tonic. The chromatic style of contemporary music makes possible the use of a literal transposition of the subject for each answer, and there is no longer a need for tonal answers. The codetta is likewise

[3]J. S. Bach: *Well-tempered Clavier, Vol I, Fugue No. 12*. From this point on this system of abbreviation will be applied to the designation of fugues from the *Well-tempered Clavier*.

unnecessary tonally, and the fact that codettas are still commonly used illustrates again their usefulness in breaking the periodic effect of a series of regularly spaced entrances. In any era, if later expositions have two or more appearances of the subject, the key relation between them is often freer, and two successive entrances in an exposition may even be in the same key, imitating at the octave.

Most first expositions have an alternating entrance order—subject, answer, subject, answer, subject, but this is not always the case. *WTC–I–12* has subject, answer, subject, and subject. The voices of the fugue always enter in some sort of pattern, common patterns being from highest to lowest, from lowest to highest, and from the inside out—that is, alto, tenor, soprano, and bass—or a pattern of tenor, alto, bass, and soprano. Whatever the order, each new voice is usually the highest or lowest at the time that it enters, so that it is easily heard.

The performance medium for which it is written has an effect on the entrance pattern of a fugue exposition. The two fugues just analyzed were written for keyboard, and therefore, each voice has the same tone color and the same potential power of climax. In any medium where the voices are unequal, the voice that is the most climactic is often reserved for the last entrance, especially in the first and last exposition. Good examples of this device are furnished by almost any organ fugue, since in the organ the bass voice can be played by the pedal keyboard, which can be coupled with a manual to create an extremely forceful sound.

If the medium is as large as an orchestra or band, the number of real parts is still small, and doublings are used. The first exposition is usually limited to four entrances of as many parts, each of which may be heavily doubled and which may change color rather rapidly. Throughout the remainder of the fugue the number of real parts remains small, but a large medium does invite some freedom of part writing, and the number of parts present at any one time may vary considerably. If a fugue is written for orchestra and chorus, it is usually complete in the chorus parts and the instruments merely double these lines. However, occasionally the instruments are called upon to play a melody which is unsuitable for voices. Examples of this are found in the double fugues by Verdi and Stravinsky discussed in a later section.

The normal first exposition lasts just long enough for each voice to enter with the subject. As was seen in *WTC–I–21*, there may be a redundant entry of the subject. There may even be two redundant entries, and some fugues have two complete expositions in the tonic key before the first development. A good example of this is *WTC–I–11* in which a second complete exposition starts in bar 18. *Counterexposition* is the term used for this second exposition in the tonic key. Usually the order of entrance of the voices is different in the first exposition and the counterexposition. Counterexpositions and redundant entries are considered as extensions of the first exposition rather than second expositions, since they continue the key pattern of the first exposition.

VARIED TREATMENTS OF THE SUBJECT

Since the subject is heard a number of times in the course of a fugue, composers often find it effective to vary the subject by applying one of the contrapuntal devices, of which the most commonly used is inversion. In some fugues the subject enters one or more times in its inverted form, either in a separate exposition or in an exposition that also contains the normal form of the subject. If this technique is to be used, the subject must be so designed that it is effective as a melody in either its original or inverted form and must be such that these two forms are readily distinguished. An entrance of an inverted subject may be found in bar 14 of *WTC–I–6*. In *WTC–II–3* the third appearance of the subject in the first exposition is inverted; this fugue makes much use of this device.

Less commonly used are the related devices of augmentation and diminution. These are most frequently found near the end of a fugue, since either device gives a feeling of climax. An augmented entry is found in *WTC–I–8* in bar 77. Diminution and augmentation are well illustrated throughout *Contrapunctus VI* and *Contrapunctus VII* of Bach's *Art of Fugue* and are used in conjunction with inversion, a common occurrence. The device of retrograde is difficult to hear and therefore is rarely used by fugue composers, since a major feature of the form is the ready detection of the presence of the subject. A fugue which uses this device very successfully for an entire exposition is the last movement of Beethoven's *Piano Sonata in B Flat, Op. 106* (Hammerclavier). All the other devices mentioned here are also found, and the entire fugue is a *tour de force* of the fugue-maker's skill.

Another device that somewhat obscures the subject is mirror.[4] The head of the subject is used in mirror in the last measure of *WTC–I–20*. The fugue from Bartók's *Music for String Instruments, Percussion and Celesta* has an exposition by mirror beginning in bar 78.

In the first exposition of a fugue, the entire subject is heard in one voice before another voice enters. This is generally also true in subsequent expositions, but sometimes for reason of climax, a second and even third entry of the subject occurs before the starting voice has completed the subject. This overlapping of subjects is called an exposition by stretto, or a *stretto*. A subject has to be specially designed to be used in stretto. A very clear example of a stretto is bar 37 of *WTC–I–11*. Here all three voices enter two bars apart at the interval of an octave. *WTC–I–1* uses stretto throughout and should be studied for its many examples of this device. A most unusual use of stretto occurs in the first exposition of *WTC–II–3*. Not only is the third entrance inverted, as mentioned earlier, but the exposition is actually in stretto, since the entrances occur at half-bar intervals although the subject is clearly a bar and a half long. One last stretto of monumental proportions must be mentioned in *WTC–I–22*. In bar 67 all five voices participate in a stretto, after which the fugue quickly comes to a close, since no further climax can be achieved. Although stretto is a device of climax, an even greater build-up can be achieved in a succession of strettos either by increasing the number of voices participating in each successive stretto or by successively shortening the time interval of the imitation. *WTC–II–5* makes use of both these techniques. The fourth entrance of the subject in the bass (bar 6) is actually in stretto, since it comes one bar after the soprano entrance instead of the bar and a half needed for the soprano to complete the subject. In bar 14 the soprano and alto present the subject at the interval of a half bar, and by the end of bar 27, in the bass and soprano parts, the time interval is reduced to a single beat. Since this is the greatest excitement that Bach can generate by shortening the time interval, he now increases the number of voices participating in the stretto from two in bar 27 to three in bar 33, to four in bar 44. This is the ultimate in stretto for this subject and the climax so produced quickly ends the fugue.

[4] The term *mirror* is used here to mean the simultaneous playing of a melody and its inversion.

MODULATING SUBJECTS

While most fugue subjects are grounded very clearly in a single key, a small number start in the tonic key and modulate to a strong cadence in another key, usually the dominant. These subjects require special handling for the answer. If a real answer is used it will modulate to the next key in the circle of fifths, and the original tonic key will not return. The common solution to this problem is to use a tonal answer which states the head of the subject literally but alters the end to modulate back to the tonic. Since the subject modulates from tonic to dominant and the answer modulates from dominant to tonic, no codetta is needed. This alteration of the answer requires a corresponding alteration of any countersubjects.

DOUBLE AND TRIPLE FUGUES

Some fugues have more than one subject. The double fugue employs two, and the triple fugue uses three. In a true double fugue the two subjects must be of equal importance as melodies and in their use, for if one subject is more important than the other the result is not a double fugue but a single fugue with a prominent countersubject. There are essentially three ways to present and use the two subjects in a double fugue. One type presents both subjects together in double counterpoint at the beginning of the fugue, in which case only one more voice enters each time so that the number of voices increase from the initial two to three and then to four. The subjects remain together in each exposition, thus insuring their equality. When two subjects are used together, it is customary to have one start a beat or so before the other so that each will be easily heard by the listener. The second type of double fugue starts with a normal exposition of a single subject, but in the second or a later exposition the second subject is added to the first and the subjects remain together for the subsequent expositions. The third type presents the first subject in the exposition, continues as a normal single fugue, and then breaks off and presents the second subject in what would also be a normal exposition of a single fugue. After development of the second subject, there comes a climactic double exposition in which the two subjects are combined. All three of these procedures insure the equality of treatment of the two subjects so necessary for a double fugue.

Two examples of the first type of double fugue are the *Kyrie* of the Mozart *Requiem* and the *Sanctus* of the Verdi *Requiem*. In both works one subject starts very shortly before the other, and in the *Sanctus* there is also a countersubject in the violins from the start. A choral fugue that illustrates the second type is the second movement of the *Symphony of Psalms* by Stravinsky. Here the fugue opens with the first subject in the orchestra, since its angular nature makes it unsuitable for the chorus. When the chorus enters it is with a second subject and the first subject is in the orchestra. After this the subjects are generally found together, but because of the nature of the two melodies the first subject is always in the orchestra and the second is in the chorus, a novel approach to the separation of subjects desirable in a double fugue. The final movement of Hindemith's *Third Piano Sonata* makes use of the third type of double fugue. The fugue starts with a four-voice exposition using the keys of B flat, F, C, and B flat. This is followed by an extensive fugue on this subject before the music pauses and an exposition of the second subject follows. This second subject, incidentally, was first heard in a somewhat different form in the third movement, where it served as the subject of a fugato. After the exposition of the second subject there is a development section using it and then another pause in the motion. This is followed by a very forceful exposition that uses both subjects in counterpoint. Both subjects, complete and in fragments, are used for the rest of the fugue, although the first subject seems slightly more important by the end of the movement.

In rare instances fugues are written with more than two subjects. *WTC–I–4* is a triple fugue of the second type. Subject one is presented at the beginning, subject two is added to the first in bar 35, and subject three is added in bar 49. The three subjects remain together until a point near the end at which there is an elaborate stretto of subject three alone. The three subjects are very different in character so that each will have a clear identity in the listener's mind. Before leaving this topic, mention must be made of the quadruple fugue in the *Art of Fugue* which was left incomplete at Bach's death (*Contrapunctus XIX*). Enough of it exists to see that it was to have been of Type 3, and that after the fourth subject, the *Art of Fugue* subject, was presented in an exposition there would have followed a monumental quadruple exposition.

THE DEVELOPMENT SECTIONS

As in any other form, it is difficult to generalize about the many occurrences in a development section. A few very brief observations can be made, but it is difficult to say whether these are typical of fugue, or of Bach as a composer and of the style and techniques of the time in which he lived. Developments are modulatory by nature, since they must start in one key and end in other. They are based on material from the subject and countersubjects, free material found in the first exposition, or more rarely, new material introduced in a development, generally the first. Much of this thematic relationship consists of the use of motives, and the need for strong, concise motives in the subject and countersubjects of a fugue cannot be overemphasized. Development sections make great use of sequence, both melodic and harmonic, and sometimes very elaborate patterns are produced. Since expositions tend to use all the voices, developments may provide some variety in texture by employing a fewer number of parts. The best method of going beyond these generalizations in a study of developments is the analysis of a number of them.

FUGATO

One of the most consistent features of fugue form is the strictly organized first exposition, and it is not surprising that composers sometimes use a fugue exposition as a section within a larger, non-fugal work. Such a passage is called a *fugato*. This is a strictly organized exposition with several entrances of the subject and often with countersubjects. The subject and sometimes the countersubject will consist of thematic material from the piece in which the fugato occurs, and this fugal treatment of the material is one method of development. This device is particularly common in music of the twentieth century because of the increased importance of counterpoint and contrapuntal techniques.

The slow movement of the *Seventh Symphony* of Beethoven has two examples of fugato. The first is the elaborate passage that first presents the first theme (bars 3 through 98). The 24-bar fugue subject is presented by the violas and then imitated by the second violins, first violins, and winds. After presenting the subject, the violas then present two countersubjects which are also carried through the other parts, this process continuing during subsequent appearances of the theme. Two features are found in this fugato that are not common in fugue–the initial harmonization of the subject and the fact that the four entrances are at the octave and therefore all in the tonic key. The other fugato in this piece, bar 183, develops the main theme. Here a sixteenth-note countersubject accompanies the subject from the start, so that the texture will not drop to one voice. The four string sections each have one entrance in the usual subject–answer relationship. Both of these examples demonstrate how a four-voice fugue may be scored for symphony orchestra.

In Stravinsky's *Octet* the last of the variations in the slow movement is a fugato. At number 51 the fugue subject is in the first bassoon accompanied by the second bassoon. The answer, in the clarinet, is in the dominant, and the third entrance, at number 52 in the first trumpet, is in the tonic. A second answer in the flute and clarinet comes at 53, after which there is a development until the third bar of 54, where the second trumpet has the head of the subject. The fugal passage then dissolves into a transition to the last movement.

THE GENERAL DESIGN OF A FUGUE

The general form of fugue as a series of expositions and developments moving through a series of keys is only one possibility in the design of a fugue. If all pieces called fugue were considered, as well as such antecedent forms to the fugue as the *canzona* and *ricercar*, the variety of forms would be overwhelming. It is beyond the scope of this work to attempt such a study, but some observations about other patterns of fugal pieces are in order.

A common alternative form is to construct the fugue of a series of expositions, each of which may have a different subject, and have no development sections at all. In this case the number of entrances of a subject will not be limited to the number of voices, but rather there will be quite an elaborate imitation of the subject. A clear example of this technique is the *Canzona in F Major* by Frescobaldi.[5] Each of the expositions in this canzona is separate from the others and has a distinct character. Each contains its own subject, there being no attempt to return material in a later part of the composition. A common variant of this procedure is one in which the subjects of the successive expositions are not unrelated melodies, but rather variations of the initial subject. This is clearly demonstrated by a *Canzona Francese* by Trabaci.[6] This technique may, in turn, be varied by using the same form of the subject for two or more expositions, but using a different countersubject in each exposition. In either case a relationship is maintained between the expositions. The two canzonas just referred to have a series of clearly separated sections instead of the continuous flow of the form found in the fugues previously studied. But this aspect of form may also vary from piece to piece. Beyond the suggestion of these possibilities, a study of the varieties of fugal forms is best undertaken from a more distinctly historical point of view.

As a final illustration of the variety possible in the construction of a fugue, two fugues will be examined whose form does not depend upon the alternation of exposition and development but rather upon elaborate patterns of imitation and treatment of the subject.

J. S. Bach: *Well–tempered Clavier, Vol. I—Fugue No. 20 in A Minor*

This fugue contains no developments as such, and even the technique of separating the successive expositions by having a new key center for each is not used. Rather there is an elaborate imitative treatment of the subject involving the use of inversion and stretto, and each successive exposition is identified by a new version of these treatments.

This four-voice fugue starts with a straightforward exposition of the subject which comes to an end on the first beat of bar 14. Instead of a development at this point, there immediately follows an exposition in which each voice states the inversion of the subject—soprano in bar 14, tenor in bar 18, bass in bar 21, and alto

[5] Archibald T. Davidson and Willi Apel, *Historical Anthology of Music, Vol. II* (Cambridge, Mass.: Harvard University Press, 1950), No. 194.

[6] *Ibid.*, No. 191.

in bar 24. Notice that the order of entrances of the voices is different in this exposition from that of the first exposition. Each successive exposition likewise has a new order of entrance for the various voices, so that there is constant variety in this respect. This second exposition ends on the third beat of bar 27, and there follows at once a third exposition which starts with an entrance in stretto of the original subject in the soprano and tenor voice. This is followed by three more pairs of entrances in stretto in first the alto and bass, next the tenor and alto, and finally the soprano and bass. These four pairs of entrances are the equivalent of the four single entrances in the earlier expositions. This exposition ends in the middle of bar 46, and in bar 48 there begins a fourth exposition in which there is again stretto, this time applied to the interverted form of the subject. Here the four pairs are alto and tenor, bass and soprano, soprano and alto, and bass and tenor, although this last is incomplete. The fifth exposition starts in bar 65 and makes use of both the original form of the subject and the inverted form. Here the paired entrances are bass and tenor, soprano and alto, bass and alto, and alto and soprano, again with the last incomplete. The final step in the treatment of these two forms of the subject is the use of both in a four-part stretto (bar 83). Here again the subjects are not complete. The two forms of the subject are continued to the end, and the last bar contains the head of both in mirror.

Clearly in this fugue the successive expositions are defined by the four entries of some new treatment of the subject, not by the key pattern, and Bach uses an unusual key pattern to obtain an interplay between it and the exposition plan. Obviously when a fugue is based on such an elaborate treatment of the subject, the composition of the subject is an extremely critical undertaking. For this reason it is logical to assume that the subject must have been written after the general design of the fugue took shape so that it would fulfill all that it was required to do.

Bartók: *Music for String Instruments, Percussion, and Celesta—1st Movement*

This movement carries fugue in fifths to its logical conclusion. All else in the design is subordinate to the successive entrances of the subject in the circle of fifths. The subject is presented first by the violas in the tonic key of A, and continues to the first note of bar

5, starting and ending on its keynote. The violins then present a normal dominant answer, but the third entrance is not the usual tonic subject but rather a subdominant answer. This is in the cellos, below the original viola entrance. This pair of answers, one above in the dominant and one below in the subdominant, introduces the scheme of the entire fugue. There are a number of entrances of the subject, some above and some below, the upper series moving to the sharp side of the circle of fifths and the lower series moving to the flat side. These two circles finally both reach the most distant key from A, the key of E flat. Here they again join, as can be seen in the first half of the diagram in Example 90. From this midpoint the upper series continues to move to the sharp side until it returns to the key of A and the lower series continues its motion until it, too, reaches A. This return to tonic brings the fugue to an end.

EXAMPLE 90: Diagram of the Fugue from Bartók: *Music for String Instruments, Percussion, and Celesta*

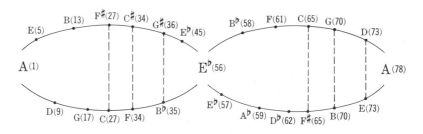

$- - -$ indicates stretto

After the entrance of all five voices, there is a short six-bar development lasting until bar 27, where there is an exposition by stretto. The first and second violins have the F sharp entrance of the upper chain, and the cellos and basses have the C entrance of the lower chain. This is followed by a double stretto. In the upper series there is an entrance of the C sharp subject in the second violins in bar 34 followed by the first violins an octave higher in bar 35. At the same time the lower series is continued by entrances in F in the violas in bar 34 and the third and fourth violins in bar 35. These subjects are not all complete, and from this point Bartók rarely uses the full length of the subject. The final stretto before the middle of the fugue occurs in bars 35 and 36 with a B flat entry in the cellos and a G sharp entry in the violas. Following this there is a long development based on the fugue subject that builds to the climax at bar 56. At bar 45, in the first and second violins, an E flat entry of the subject is heard, but passes almost unnoticed.

From the first moment that two parts sound together, the harmony of this fugue is very rich and complex. As the climactic midpoint is approached, the tension of the harmony increases to the point where more rich chords could have little effect. Therefore, Bartók achieves his climax by a sudden and very dramatic decrease in tension—the octave E flats in bar 56. Clearly achieving a climax depends not so much upon great increases in harmonic tension as upon changes in tension, whether increases or decreases. Immediately the lower voices make an entrance of the subject in inversion in E flat, and this and the subject in the same key in the violins (bar 45) gives each circle of entrances an E flat entrance. The inverted form of the subject, used for the first time in bar 57, is used for the expositions in the second half of the fugue to provide an element of contrast between the two halves. From here on the suggestions of the subject are more fragmentary, since the subject and the pattern of its use are more apparent. The octave B flats in bar 58 represent this key in the upper chain, and in bar 59 the cellos and basses make the A flat entrance in the lower chain. Likewise in bar 61 the octave F's present that key in the upper chain. This means that the cello and bass part that follows should be the D flat entrance for the lower chain, yet this entrance starts on B flat. However, an examination of the inverted form of the fugue subject starting on the note D flat (Example 91) will show that this cello-bass part is essentially the last phrase of the fugue subject, as indicated by the bracket.

EXAMPLE 91:   Bartók: *Music for String Instruments, Percussion, and Celesta*

An immediate reaction to this discovery is to suspect that Bartók made this entrance obscure to test the skill of the analysts. Actually, there is a very good musical reason for his procedure here. As in the case of the A flat entrance in the lower chain in bar 59, the entrance comes while the octaves that were the upper entrance are still sounding. Thus the D flat entrance must come under a sustained octave F. If the beginning of the D flat fugue subject seen in Example 91 were played with the note F, a very obvious F major triad would result, a chord of too low tension to be used at this point in the piece. Hence the use of a later fragment of the subject which produces a more satisfactory harmony.

The rest of the entries are clearer. C above and F sharp below are found in the first and second violins in bar 65 and alternate in stretto so that there are six entrances in all. Bar 70 brings G above and B below, and bar 73 brings D above in the second violin and E below in the cello. This brings both circles back to the tonic key of A. The two forms of the subject are presented in the tonic in the exposition by mirror in bar 78. A final imitation of the two forms of the head of the subject leads to a final mirror of the subject head which ends the fugue on a unison A.

The unusual nature of the D flat entrance in the returning chain just discussed illustrates an important point that is worthy of further consideration. The plan of this fugue is very simple and direct and at the same time highly organized. Yet at this point a slavish following of the dictates of the plan would have produced a harmony which would have weakened the musical expression of the fugue. Given this problem, Bartók, or any other great composer, will abandon a literal following of the plan rather than weaken the expression of the composition. Thus the greatness of a piece of music, or of any other work of art, depends on its expression, not upon the technical perfection of its design. Examples of modification of a preconceived plan in the interest of expression are common in music, and are nowhere more common than in the fugues of Bach. This is important to keep in mind, since Bach is so much studied as a master of structure and technique.

EXAMPLES FOR ANALYSIS

A study of fugue should begin with the study of many of the fugues of the first volume of the *Well-tempered Clavier* of Bach. This should certainly include the *C Major, C Sharp Major* and *Minor, D Minor, E Flat Major, E Minor, F Major, F Minor, G Minor, A Flat Major,* and *B Flat Minor,* although not necessarily in that order. Further study should involve the fugues of the second volume and other Baroque fugues. All the examples referred to in the text can be explored more thoroughly with profit, especially those mentioned in the section on double fugues. A few more recent fugues are suggested below to bring the study of the subject up to date.

Franck: *Prelude, Chorale, and Fugue*

Hindemith: *Ludus Tonalis* (Twelve fugues are included within this work)

Stravinsky: *Concerto per due Pianoforte Soli—4th Movement, Preludio e Fuga*

Barber: *Sonata for Piano, Op. 26—Finale*

X

Variation Forms

A PIECE of music is more intensely expressive if it is based on a small amount of melodic material. Two basic techniques for creating a long work from a few basic musical ideas have been studied: the practice of recapitulating material after an intervening contrasting passage, and the process of development. This chapter discusses a third basic technique for this same purpose, the process of variation. Few practices have had a longer or more fruitful history, and the term must be understood to cover a variety of practices. Many aspects of this form will be considered, and from these the basic nature of the variation process will become apparent.[1]

The problem of devising a system of classification that encompasses the great variety of works of the variation type is a complex one and cannot be completely solved. Any such system will never

---

[1] As in the case of fugue, the subject of variation is worthy of far more study than is possible in a single chapter. The reader is referred to *The Technique of Variation* by Robert U. Nelson, (Berkeley: University of California Press, 1949).

be completely satisfactory, and the one used here must be considered only a partial solution. The first basic division of variations is into two types—separate variations and continuous variations. In the first group are all those variations in which the theme is a separate piece, since in this case the variations must also be separate from one another. Into the second group go those pieces that flow without pause from variation to variation, with no harmonic ending for any one variation.

SEPARATE VARIATIONS

These may also be called by the general title of *theme and variations*. It must be understood that the theme is not necessarily a melody, as the name suggests, but rather a small piece of music. A theme and variations starts with a small, complete piece of music called the *theme*. This piece is formally complete and capable of standing alone, and ends with a feeling of finality. It is usually in a small form, binary form being used far more than ternary. This is not surprising considering that in ternary form the first and third sections are alike. Clearly this form would become tedious if it were found in every variation. The variations that follow the theme both differ from it in some way and have some area of contact with it. In addition each variation is unique, although some may be similar for reasons that will be seen later.

The basic relationship between the theme and each of the variations consists of preserving the basic harmonic structure of the theme, including the rhythmic pattern of the harmony. This means that the phrase and sentence structure of the theme, and indeed its very form, are contained in each variation. Each variation is therefore small and complete like the theme, and ends with the same cadence. The name *theme and variations* is misleading if it is taken to mean that the melody of the theme section will remain constant, for it is rather the harmonic scheme and form that are constant. Some sets of variations preserve every detail of the harmony in each variation, but some retain only the main outline and basic chords and change the details considerably. Sometimes a new chord is substituted for one of the same basic type, such as submediant for tonic or mediant for dominant, but until the twentieth century the preservation of the harmonic pattern provided the basic link between the theme and each variation. Because of the development of a much more complex harmonic style in this century, this is no longer true, and theme and variation is one form for which the examples of our own century must be discussed separately.

The variations may have further points of similarity with the theme. The most common of these is a melodic relationship, and many variations contain a somewhat more florid or otherwise altered version of the melody of the theme. The harmonic relationship may also involve the use of the same chord inversions and hence result in the same bass line. Beyond these general observations, a discussion of the variety of variations possible is beyond the scope of this chapter.

As a set of variations is analyzed, each variation must be examined to see all possible relationships that it may have with the theme, and also to discover what is new and distinctive about it. Each variation of a set has some idea that is unique to it, and it is often dominated by this idea. It may be a new rhythmic idea, a new mood, or a new treatment of the melody of the theme; but whatever it is, each variation is given an individuality. Since the harmonic pattern is repeated in each variation, the form of the theme is found in each variation and need not be analyzed. However, any repeated strains in the theme should be noted, since these repeats may be written out in some variations. Sometimes such written-out repeats are varied so that different forms of the repeated strain are found within one variation.

One basic aspect of the theme-and-variation form is the forward movement felt as the piece progresses. The variations are written to be played in a definite order, and the composer takes advantage of this fact to create certain effects as the variations pass. One common practice is to generate increasing rhythmic excitement. If the basic melodic motion of the theme were in quarter notes, then the first variation might move in eighth notes, the second in eighth-note triplets, and the third in sixteenth notes. There is obviously a limit to this technique, but it may be extended by having the faster rhythmic motion not in successive variations but in separated ones. Another common device for drawing the listener forward in the form is to have the first variation closely and directly related to the theme, the second slightly less related, and so on, until a variation appears whose connection with the theme is very tenuous. This is the most successful if each new variation grows very logically out of the immediately preceding one, so that the connection from variation to variation is always clear to the listener. A set of variations of this sort will have an occasional variation that is much more like the theme than the variations that preceded it, as if to reestablish the listener's contact with the theme. This practice also suggests a return to the opening of the work, almost in the nature of a recapitulation, which adds the principle of departure and return to the technique of theme and variation. This suggests a larger organization of the variations into groups, and such is sometimes the case. Several successive variations may have a common element such as the same mode, tempo, or mood, and thus combine into a larger section. This purposeful flow from variation to variation does much to counteract the disjointed effect that a number of small, separate pieces would have.

In some sets of variations, successive variations present completely contrasting moods or natures, and the contrast between them is great. These are deserving of special note, since the degree of separation is extreme. As might be expected, such variations are mainly a product of the Romantic composers of the nineteenth century, although isolated examples occur before that time, notably the *Goldberg Variations* of Bach. Some contemporary variations are of this sort, as will be seen in the analysis of the second movement of Stravinsky's *Octet*.

A theme and its variations form a complete piece which may stand alone or may be used as a movement within a larger work. If the variations stand alone, there may be an introduction or a conclusion to add a sense of completeness. Sometimes a climactic coda is added, and sometimes a fugue, using the theme as its subject, is used to finish out a set of variations. Brahms in his *Haydn Variations* uses a set of continuous variations as a finale to a theme and variations. If a theme-and-variations form is found within a longer piece, it is most often used for the slow movement. However, reference should be made to the use of variations as finales by both Haydn and Mozart, not to mention Beethoven, who used theme and variations for the finales of both the *Eroica* and *Ninth Symphony*.

There are several common sources for the piece that serves as the theme for variation. It may have been composed expressly for the set of variations that it produces, or it may have been written for another piece by the composer. The theme may not even be by the composer of the variations, in which case a sort of musical collaboration takes place, although the main task of composition is the creation of the variations, and the finished piece is known by their composer's name. When two names are given, as in the Brahms *Haydn Variations* mentioned earlier, the use of Haydn's name is merely a convenient way to identify this set of variations, since Brahms wrote only one on a theme by Haydn. Some themes have attracted more than one composer, a notable one being the theme of a *Caprice* by Paganini which has resulted in sets of variations by such composers as Brahms, Liszt, Rachmaninoff, Boris Blacher, and, of course, Paganini himself.

Beethoven: *Piano Sonata in A Flat, Op. 26—Andante con Variationi*

This set of variations is the first movement of the sonata, and is based on a theme which was written for this work. Any consideration of a set of variations must begin with a very thorough analysis of the theme, since so much will grow from it. In this case, the theme is that type of small form with both binary and ternary characteristics that was discussed in Chapter II. It consists of four sentences, of which the first, second, and fourth are similar. The third sentence is distinctly different. Further, the first sentence ends with a half cadence and the second with a full cadence, so that they are bound together as a double sentence. As in any theme and variations, a thorough analysis of the theme must include a complete harmonic analysis, so that any change in the harmonic pattern in any variation may be discovered.

Each variation of this set has an individual melodic pattern, and in the first variation the melody of the theme is readily discovered in this pattern. The first sentence and the others that are like it use an arpeggio of four thirty-second notes on the first beat of each measure. The third sentence, which in the theme and in each variation is the contrasting one, shifts this arpeggio to the left hand and sometimes extends it. The harmonic pattern of the theme is followed exactly. This is also true in the second variation, with the exception of a dominant of the subdominant chord added in the last beat of the fourth bar and at corresponding places throughout the variation. The melody of the theme is clearly suggested in this variation by the left-hand part, and the relentless thirty-second note rhythm produced by an alternation of hands, carries throughout the variation. From the theme through the first two variations there is an increase of rhythmic activity, a common technique.

The third variation offers a contrast, for it is in the minor mode, and the melody of the theme is only suggested, not quoted. Again there is an alternation of notes between the two hands, but here the resulting rhythm is sixteenth notes instead of thirty-second notes. This slower rhythm, plus the minor mode, creates a more somber mood. The only vestige of the theme remaining is an upward motion suggestive of the general melodic outline of the theme. The greatest departure from the theme, however, is in the harmonic pattern. Beethoven is not content merely to shift the harmonies of the theme into the minor mode, but rather reworks the harmonic pattern to make it more suitable to the minor mode, thus, effecting a very basic change in the expression. From the third bar on, the harmony is only vaguely related to what has come before, and such changes as the introduction of a Neapolitan sixth chord in the fourth bar, a dominant of the subdominant in the fifth bar, and the subdominant in the sixth bar are common. The third sentence is likewise changed: the dominant of the supertonic and supertonic, used in the theme to start this sentence, are now replaced by a subdominant chord preceded by its dominant. The changes made in the first sentence are also found in the second and fourth sentences. However, the very basic elements of the harmonic pattern of the theme, such as the half cadence at the end of the first sentence, the full cadences at the end of the second and fourth, and the secondary chords and their secondary dominants in the third sentence are carefully preserved.

With the fourth variation the mode returns to major, but the harmony again bears only a basic resemblance to that of the theme. The rhythmic motion of the first sentence is again eighth notes, and the melody, which bears a noticeable resemblance to the theme, makes use of the tied note across the bar that was introduced in the first variation and used also in the third. The second sentence would normally be a repetition of the first, but here Beethoven uses a variant of the first sentence, introducing sixteenth-note motion in the left hand. This is the practice mentioned earlier of using repetition to present two different versions of the same passage in a variation, and hence, in a sense, a variation within a variation.

Since the two variations just seen have made little direct reference to the melody of the theme, the fifth and last variation presents this melody much more literally, particularly in the second and fourth sentences. The harmony of the theme is also returned exactly, except that the dominant of the subdominant first introduced in the second variation at the end of the fourth measure is found also in this variation. Since this is the last variation of the set, Beethoven felt the need of a more conclusive ending, and this is supplied by a fifteen-bar coda.

A larger organization of the form can be seen in this movement. The first two variations present the melody of the theme in an obvious figured pattern with ever-increasing rhythmic motion and exact repetitions of the harmony. The next two variations change the mood considerably, slow the rhythmic motion, and alter the details of the harmony. The last variation returns the harmony, mood, and melody of the theme, almost giving a feeling of recapitulation. However, these observations about the over-all form of the movement are drawn from the music itself, and it is impossible to predict from them the general plan of another set of variations. Each set is approached as a new problem by the composer, and new solutions to the problem of organization are created. Likewise, it is impossible to predict all the various ways in which a variation may differ from its theme, and the ingenuity of composers in writing many different variations on a theme is constantly apparent.

One more form of separate variations should be discussed. The first major examples of this form are found in the music of Haydn, and it was used in turn by Beethoven, although it did not seem to interest his successors. This form consists of using not one, but two themes for a set of variations. For this reason this practice can be called *variations on a double theme*. Haydn usually separated the two themes in the listener's mind by shifting mode. Thus in his *Andante Varie in F Minor* for piano, and also in the slow movement of his *Symphony No. 103 in E Flat* (Drumroll), the first theme is a complete small form in the minor mode, which is followed by a second complete piece in the major mode. These can be called Theme One and Theme Two, since they do not share any melodic material. Following the presentation of the two themes comes Variation One on the first theme, Variation One on the second theme, and so on as long as the set of variations lasts. The shift of mode between each new theme or variation makes a clear separation between the sections. A set of variations on a double theme will not have many variations of each theme, lest too long a movement result. Beethoven's greatest contribution to this form is the slow movement of his *Ninth Symphony* (Choral). The organization is the same as that of the pieces by Haydn just discussed, expect that the separation between the two themes is achieved not by use of opposite modes, but rather by the use of a slow theme in duple meter followed by a faster theme in triple meter. This shift of meter from duple to triple is also common in Beethoven's other variations on double themes.

A similar term, but one that designates a different practice, is *double variation*. This technique is possible only in themes in which there is a repeated strain. It consists of writing out and varying this repeat so that it is really varied twice. Thus a double variation occurs within a single numbered variation. Brahms was a master of this technique, as he was of all aspects of variation writing.

In most sets of variations each variation is in the tonic key, although the shift of mode seen in the Beethoven movement is quite common. Therefore, the only tonal variety is provided by the modulations that are found within the theme itself, since these will necessarily be a part of the harmonic content of each variation. To avoid the relentless tonality of a long set of variations, composers do sometimes write occasional variations in some other key. If this happens, the shift of tonality from variation to variation may also be used to create a larger organization of the work.

CONTEMPORARY THEME AND VARIATIONS

The greatly expanded harmonic resources and techniques of the twentieth century have had a great effect on the theme and variations. It is difficult to conceive of a small binary form with a simple harmonic structure in today's style. Furthermore, the harmonic pattern would not be as memorable because of the vast possibilities of twentieth-century harmony. The themes of earlier centuries used the most basic harmonies, so that the presence of these harmonies in each variation could be readily felt. Thus the theme-and-variations form could not come into this century without some basic changes in its nature. It is an indication of the vitality of this form and of its continued usefulness to composers that it has undergone the changes necessary to make it valid in the style of this century, instead of merely being abandoned. Curiously enough, since modern composers are not able to depend on the harmonic pattern of the theme to provide a sure link between it and the variations, they have come to depend more on the melody of the theme to provide this connection, thus creating works that more closely live up to the name, *theme and variations* than do those of the past. The practice of making the theme and each of the variations a separate entity has continued, and the general term *separate variations* is as appropriate as ever. Since in contemporary examples the variations do not necessarily follow the exact form of the theme, the form of each variation must be analyzed separately. Often these formal variants throw further light on the formal implications of the theme. Two twentieth-century sets of variations are discussed here. These demonstrate to some extent common contemporary variation procedures, but the details of the relation between the theme and a variation are worked out more individually today, and it is less possible than ever to generalize about the process.

Prokofiev: *Piano Concerto No. 3, Op. 26—2nd Movement*

Theme: The theme consists of four four-bar phrases, the first and last of which are alike, making a ternary form. The two middle phrases each have a distinct idea, so the form of the theme can be expressed as A B C A. Ternary is quite a common form for a variation theme, since contemporary composers seem to prefer not to write binary forms. The theme ends with a two-chord cadence in the winds, which is also used to end each variation.

Variation I: Since the orchestra presented the theme, the soloist is featured in the first variation. The piano alone plays the theme, and in Sections A and B the only alteration is the repetition of the third bar of the theme, which is heard three times instead of once. Section C is presented as a florid series of arpeggios, and the piano continues this passage work while the woodwinds present the second appearance of A.

Variation II: This variation brings an abrupt shift of mood. The piano and orchestra leap into an agitated passage which turns out to be a setting for the theme. Section A of the theme is played by the trumpet and B by the high strings and woodwinds. Section C follows in an eighth-note figuration, after which the trumpet again plays A, this time with certain notes greatly elongated. The use of the trumpet to present the A section each time greatly contributes to the feeling of ternary form as the structure of this variation.

Variation III: The first part of this variation is dominated by a driving figure in the piano that is derived from section A of the theme and represents it in this variation. While the triplet motion continues in the piano, the high woodwinds play section B of the theme, after which the piano is again featured with the driving motion of A. The high woodwinds play section C, again accompanied by the rushing triplets in the piano, and the variation then ends with the A section a third time in the piano. Because of the insertion of A between B and C, the form of this variation is A B A C A. Note the parallel scoring in the various sections. Much of the character of this variation is imparted by the driving version of section A of the theme and it seems likely that Prokofiev used it an extra time to heighten the effect.

Variation IV: This variation gives the effect of being a slow movement in a multimovement work, so different have the tempos of the variations been. We hear first a flowing version of the first two bars of section A, which is immediately repeated. The piano and orchestra then alternate in a presentation of section B, after which A is heard once again. This variation follows the form of the last one, and the placid version of section A, which is heard three times, sets the mood of the variation. Section C, when it finally does appear, does little to alter this mood.

Variation V: This is the last variation and it uses quite a different formal technique than any used before. The variation starts with a melody in the piano which is based on the dotted pick-up notes and the leap up a fourth that started the theme. This figure is thoroughly exploited for 19 bars, after which the violins enter with a figure based on the first two bars of section B. This, in turn, is developed and is used to attain a climax, after which the orchestra becomes gradually softer until the theme is suddenly recapitulated very literally. The cadence at the end of the theme is extended to make an ending for the movement. This last variation never presents the melody of the theme, but rather develops two characteristic motives from it. At the same time, it is the longest of the variations, and the one that reaches the greatest climax. The method of construction of this variation has no connection with the form of the theme.

Several common techniques of contemporary variations are evident in the last example and are worthy of comment. The form of the theme is altered at will, some sections being heard more often in the variation than in the theme, and some not being heard at all. In the second variation the theme was present as a melody played by a prominent instrument of the orchestra, and the piano and orchestra furnished a setting for this melody—a process also evident in the next example. Furthermore, the setting started before the theme appeared, thus lengthening the variation and setting its mood. Finally, the last variation was no variation at all in the usual sense, but rather a development of ideas contained in the theme. This is a very common technique today, and one that yields much variety within a single set of variations, since the process of development can produce great variety.

Stravinsky: *Octet—Tema con Variazioni*

This set of variations occupies the traditional position as the slow movement in this work. Stravinsky labels his variations with letters instead of the usual numbers, perhaps because the first variation returns almost like the theme of a rondo. The form of the movement is Theme – Variation A – Variation B – Variation A – Variation C – Variation D – Variation A – Variation E. This last is not a variation at all, but rather a fugue, a form often used to end a set of variations. Variation A will be analyzed only once, although on each appearance the ending of the variation is slightly altered.

Theme: The theme is very simply presented, first by the flute and clarinet two octaves apart, and then by a trumpet followed by a trombone. The setting is chordal, but since it is the melody of the theme that is to give rise to the variations, it is necessary to make a thorough study of it to discover all its inner relationships before the structure of the variations will become clear. In Example 92 the theme is shown with its motivic structure analyzed. The first three fragments present three versions of the same motive, but the first is sufficiently different from the second two to stand out. It is this first version that is used later. A second and distinctly different motive follows, and after motive A returns, motive B is found twice more. The actual form of the theme has a chameleon-like nature. Looked at one way, it can be seen as a ternary form with the first two sections as part A, the next two as part B, and what follows as the return of A, since the point where the trumpet enters is certainly a return of the opening. From another point of view, the point where the trumpet enters is the middle of the theme, and each half of the theme is similar, since each presents first motive A and then motive B. Perhaps this can then be heard as a binary form. It seems foolish to suggest that the same simple melody can be heard as two distinctly different forms, depending on how it is contemplated, but this is exactly how Stravinsky heard it, and both these interpretations of the form will be seen in the variations that follow. The theme is analyzed in Example 92, with the motivic groups marked. For convenience of reference, the two-bar motives will be called Section One of the theme, Section Two, and so forth.

EXAMPLE 92:   Stravinsky: *Octet—Theme*

Variation A: In the first four bars of this variation, the theme is in the trombone parts. The turn has been eliminated, the note values are all quarter notes, and some notes are displaced an octave, as is so common when a theme or motive is quoted in contemporary music. Above this a series of thirty-second-note scales rise and fall, which are more prominent than the theme itself. The next four bars present the third and fourth sections of the theme, contained in the off beats in the flute and first trumpet, and accompanied by a reiterated descending scale in the two bassoons. The variation ends with the next two sections of the theme. Since the first of these is like the opening of the theme, Stravinsky uses the same setting that opened the variation to create a very definite ternary form. The variation ends with a statement of the B motive. Both the way the theme is quoted and the way the setting is changed in the middle section emphasize the ternary interpretation of the theme.

Variation B: This is an extended variation that contains an elaborate setting for the theme. In some places the theme seems to be of secondary importance to the setting, and there are long stretches in which the theme is not present at all. So that the theme will be apparent when it is present, Stravinsky scores it in the trumpet parts, although it is sometimes imitated by other instruments. The repeated-chord accompaniment begins the variation, after which the second trumpet plays an extended version of the first section of the theme. One bar before number 29 the first trumpet plays the second section. The theme is now dropped until four bars before number 30 where the next two sections are played by the first trumpet, again in extended form. At number 30 the two trumpets play the fifth section of the theme, and again the setting that opened the variation is returned, creating another ternary form. The last two sections of the theme, both motive B, are completely missing, but since this motive occurs earlier in the theme, no element of the theme is really eliminated. After all vestiges of the theme have vanished, there is a brief closing passage.

Variation C: This is the same type of variation as Variation B, but the setting of the theme is even more elaborate. Were the theme not present, this would seem to be a new and separate piece with its own themes. To help the hearer perceive the theme in such an elaborate setting, Stravinsky again gives it to the trumpet, this time always the second player. A new formal attitude toward the theme is apparent. The theme first enters at number 34 and the first, second, and fourth sections of it are found, the last of these coming in just before 35. The omission of the third section is no loss in completeness, since it is simply another version of motive A. Now the theme drops out until the sixth bar after number 35, and when it reenters, the new form is apparent. To return to the discussion of the structure of the theme, remember that one way to look at it is as made up of two halves, each of which uses first motive A and then motive B. This is the attitude that Stravinsky now takes toward the theme, which he shows by simply using the same trumpet part a second time with one insignificant change. This suggests a repeated strain or, if the change in the setting is noted, a binary form. Whatever it seems to be, the structure is certainly that of two parts that are equal, not the three-part structure employed for the other variations.

Variation D: This variation follows the last one directly, and the connection is made clearer by the second bassoon, which has the same arpeggio just before and after number 38. As in the recent variations, an elaborate setting is started and the theme appears in the trumpets. The theme is most often in the trumpets or some other brass, and it is apparent that Stravinsky depends on the instrumentation to help the listener follow the appearances of the theme. The first section of the theme is at 39, the second at 40, and the fourth four bars after 41. The setting then continues for so long with no sign of the theme that it seems as if Stravinsky has forgotten it. At last, at number 47, the fifth section of the theme appears in the first trumpet, after which the variation comes gradually to an end.

Variation E is not a variation at all, but rather a fugato, a form that has already been discussed. The general observation that needs to be made about this set of variations is that the theme is quoted as a melody either literally or thinly disguised, and is accompanied by an elaborate setting. These settings are really little pieces, each having its own themes, meter, tempo, and mood, so that the theme can really be said to create several independent pieces. As a procedure for writing variations, this technique is new to this century, but there are certain connections with *cantus firmus* compositions and the third type of chorale prelude that will become apparent when these are studied. Although a contemporary formal technique may seem at first to be new and unrelated to the past, further examination will often show a very real contact with past music. The contemporary composer has a greater opportunity to see the music of any period than composers have ever had before, and it is not surprising that he is influenced by what he finds.

CONTINUOUS VARIATIONS

In this type of variation the set is so connected together that a continuously flowing piece results, rather than the series of sections that characterize the other type. One means of accomplishing this effect is to have the theme so constructed that it has no strong ending, but rather uses the start of the first variation as its ending. This means that the first variation will, in turn, connect to the second, and so on throughout the variations. As well as using this type of ending, continuous variations use an unusual sort of theme, which is as basic to this type of variation as is its continuous nature. Actually, the themes used for continuous variations are of two sorts, and these will be discussed separately.

The first type of continuous variation uses as its theme a bass melody. These variations often start with this melody alone, after which it is repeated over and over while new music is put above it. The constant element in this sort of variation is the continuously repeating bass, which is called a *ground bass*, or *basso ostinato*. Sometimes the first term is shortened to *ground*. The designation variation comes from the ever-changing material above. Since the continuing bass is a melody, it seems natural to add other melodies above it, and ground bass variations are usually written in a polyphonic style. It is customary to use a single musical idea to construct each variation, which gives the necessary unity to a variation. If the theme is heard alone first, its appearance can be called the theme and what follows is Variation One. If, as is often the case, the work starts with the theme in the bass with a setting above, this is generally called the first variation and what follows is Variation Two. Analysts are not always consistent in numbering the variations, and any discussion of this type of variation must make its numbering procedure clear. The theme, or ground, for this type of continuous variation is a strong bass melody which provides for a number of very basic chord progressions. Generally, a ground is rather static rhythmically and the variations provide most of the motion, but once in a while a ground is very active, sometimes more so than any idea in the variations. In the simplest approach to this form, the ground is repeated literally in the bass voice throughout the work, but sometimes the melody of the ground moves to an upper voice, even the soprano, and sometimes it is subjected to small changes.

In the other type of continuous variation there is no repeated bass, but rather a series of chords which is repeated for each variation. Since such a chord pattern need have no single melody associated with it, it is customary to refer to the first appearance of the chord pattern as the first variation, and the next as Variation Two. The chord pattern may be as simple as two alternating chords, or it may be a complex one several measures long, but like the theme in the ground-bass variation, the ending and beginning of the chord pattern will connect so that the variations are continuous. This type of variation is also usually found in a contrapuntal style, since most of the examples of it come from the eras of polyphonic music.

It is an oversimplification to treat these two types as mutually exclusive. A ground bass tends to dictate the chords that go above it, and a series of chords that has the same inversions will have basically the same bass melody. Thus it is not alway possible to separate the two types. Moreover, the repetition of both the bass and the basic harmonies makes a stronger piece than the use of either one alone. In connection with the difficulty of differentiating these two types, mention must be made of the passacaglia and chaconne. These were originally dance pieces, but both came to be written as continuous variations. In each case the only vestige of the dance is the triple meter. Many attempts have been made to distinguish these two forms, a common one being to define them so that they fit the two monumental pieces by J. S. Bach, the *Chaconne* for unaccompanied violin and the *C Minor Passacaglia* for organ. Unfortunately, other Baroque composers were not always in agreement with the labels Bach used. If much of the literature is explored, no definition can be derived from the use of these two names which in any way distinguishes one from another. Actually, the basic principals of continuous variations are found in both types of piece, and one example will serve to illustrate the form.

J. S. Bach: *Passacaglia in C Minor for Organ*

No numbering problem exists in this work, since the theme that is the ground bass is stated by itself in the pedals, and the other parts enter at the beginning of the first variation. The theme, seen in Example 93, is eight bars long, and starts and ends on C so that, as one appearance of the theme follows another, a full bar of the note C and the tonic chord will result, thus making the harmonic flow continuous.

EXAMPLE 93: J. S. Bach: *Passacaglia in C Minor—Theme*

The texture is polyphonic, and most of the time four parts are used. Each new variation brings a fresh melodic and imitative idea, so that there is a very definite melodic separation between them.

The bass always phrases between repetitions of the ground, but the other parts phrase either before or after the break in the bass, so that at any given moment some part is continuing. This adds immeasurably to the continuous effect of the variations. The examples that are to be discussed give the first complete bar of selected variations and whatever pick-up notes preceded this bar. In the case of the theme, this is always the initial note C, but the pick-ups in the other parts vary in length. A pick-up in one part may come at the same time as the ending of the previous variation in some other part. Although for each of these variations only the beginning is given, the melodies and imitative techniques presented carry on throughout the variation.

The first variation is seen in Example 94. All three upper voices enter at once to make a simple but full harmonization of the theme.

EXAMPLE 94:   J. S. Bach: *Passacaglia in C Minor—Variation 1*

The second variation is similar to this, and then in Variation 3 imitation is introduced.

EXAMPLE 95:   J. S. Bach: *Passacaglia in C Minor—Variation 3*

As is sometimes the case in separate variations, these early variations introduce increasingly faster notes to generate rhythmic excitement. Variations 4 and 5 first introduce sixteenth notes, as can be seen in Examples 96 and 97. In Variation 5 the sixteenth notes are even applied to the theme so that the bass, too, enters into the imitation.

EXAMPLE 96: J. S. Bach: *Passacaglia in C Minor—Variation 4*

EXAMPLE 97: J. S. Bach: *Passacaglia in C Minor—Variation 5*

Variation 6 (Example 98) increases the number of sixteenth notes in a group to three, and this leads to Variation 8 (Example 99) where a long scale line of sixteenth notes is imitated.

EXAMPLE 98: J. S. Bach: *Passacaglia in C Minor—Variation 6*

EXAMPLE 99:   J. S. Bach: *Passacaglia in C Minor—Variation 8*

Example 100 presents a new technique. Here, in Variation 10, the scale line that was previously imitated is extended and remains in the soprano part while the other parts play a simple block-chord accompaniment.

EXAMPLE 100:   J. S. Bach: *Passacaglia in C Minor—Variation 10*

In Variation 12 (Example 101) the ground bass melody moves to the soprano voice, and the other parts play the variation below it.

EXAMPLE 101:   J. S. Bach: *Passacaglia in C Minor—Variation 12*

There follow several variations in which the melody of the bass is gradually submerged in florid passage work. The most extreme of these is Variation 15, and in Example 102 the vestiges of the theme can be seen in the circled notes.

EXAMPLE 102:   J. S. Bach: *Passacaglia in C Minor—Variation 15*

The next variation (Example 103) returns the original form of the theme in a chordal setting as if to make contact with it before it is lost.

EXAMPLE 103:   J. S. Bach: *Passacaglia in C Minor—Variation 16*

Example 104 shows the final stage in the increase of rhythmic excitement.

EXAMPLE 104:   J. S. Bach: *Passacaglia in C Minor—Variation 17*

The last variations are more like those that came earlier in the work, until we come to Variation 20 (Example 105) which brings the passacaglia to a close. This is followed immediately by a fugue that uses the first four bars of the ground bass as its subject. Thus the passacaglia and fugue constitute a two-movement piece based on the same melodic idea.

EXAMPLE 105: J. S. Bach: *Passacaglia in C Minor—Variation 20*

CANTUS FIRMUS

A *cantus firmus* is a pre-existent melody to which are added other parts to make a polyphonic composition. The entire melody may be found only once in a composition, in which case the form of the composition is closely related to the passage which presents the melody, or it may be repeated several times. In the latter case, the procedure is not unlike the type of variation just studied in that the cantus firmus remains constant and the other parts vary. A basic difference is that the cantus firmus is usually stated in an inner part in a rather neutral rhythm and is therefore much more obscure than a ground bass. Nonetheless, when a composition is created around a pre-existent melody which is found throughout most of the piece, its entire form is affected. These melodies have been taken from many sources, and frequently a religious melody is used as the cantus of a new religious work. Protestant composers have made much use of the chorales of their Church, since these melodies would be somewhat familiar to the congregation. In a sense, a composition that makes use of a chorale may be considered as a variation on a theme, since although the theme is not stated before the variation it has been heard at some previous time. In studying this music it is a good idea to become familiar with the melody of the chorale, since the composer expected the listener to bring this knowledge to the piece. The chorale was such an important part of the Protestant Church music of the Baroque Era that two types of pieces were developed which used it as their basis—the chorale prelude for organ, and a type of cantata based on the chorale. Although they are not true variations in the same sense as those just studied, and although they do not always use the chorale as a cantus firmus, these pieces deserve study, for they are at least related forms.

CHORALE PRELUDE

Chorale preludes vary greatly in the elaborateness of the treatment of the chorale. The various ways in which the chorale may be set form the basis for classifying chorale preludes, since the many chorale preludes in existence are so varied that no single description of the form can be applied to all. Chorale preludes are divided into three basic types according to the treatment of the chorale melody, although it should be noticed that the first two of these types must be subdivided in order to describe the form accurately.

Whatever system of classification of chorale preludes is used, examples occur which conform to more than one type, and a system of classification must be regarded only as a useful tool with which to consider the vast chorale prelude literature.

The first type of chorale prelude is essentially a setting of the chorale melody, and this melody is present nearly continuously. It may be literally stated in the top voice with the other parts making a contrapuntal setting, one that in no way obscures the melody. Such a piece is the prelude by Bach, the beginning of which is given in Example 107. A comparison of this with the melody of the chorale (Example 106) shows the melody to be unchanged.

As in this example, the voices that provide the setting for the chorale usually make use of a limited number of melodic ideas so

EXAMPLE 106: *Ach wie fluechtig, ach wie nichtig—Chorale melody*

EXAMPLE 107: J. S. Bach: *Chorale Prelude—Ach wie fluechtig, ach wie nichtig*

there is unity both in the accompanying parts and in the mood of the setting. A variant of this procedure is seen in Example 108, where the same chorale is subjected to florid figuration.

EXAMPLE 108: Georg Boehm: *Chorale Prelude—Ach wie fluechtig, ach wie nichtig*

A third approach to this type of chorale prelude consists of using the chorale melody as a cantus firmus, generally in the bass voice. In this case the chorale melody is not heard as clearly, and the setting above it becomes more important.

A second general type of chorale prelude consists of using the chorale as thematic material for some other form. The first part of the chorale may furnish the subject of a fugue or a fugato. Other phrases of the chorale may be used later in the fugue as subjects, or the fugue may contain only the opening phrase of the chorale, thus basing the work on the chorale but not quoting it in its entirety. Example 109 is the beginning of a chorale melody which is seen as a fugue subject in Example 110, page 194. In the course of this entire fugue, the fugue subject is the only fragment of the chorale used.

EXAMPLE 109: *Ein feste Burg ist unser Gott—Chorale Melody*

Fragments of the chorale may form the basis for a chorale fantasy. As the name implies, great freedom is found in these works, and they vary greatly in form. Imitation of phrases of the chorale is common, and chorale fantasies are often not unlike free fugues on the chorale. Canon is also sometimes employed in writing a chorale prelude, and if the device is used throughout, the whole prelude becomes a canon. A final form used is the theme and variation. In this form there are generally as many appearances of the chorale melody as there are verses of the text, and all the observations previously made about theme and variations apply as well to chorale variations.

A third type of chorale prelude must be distinguished, although strictly speaking it contains no new techniques, but rather uses those of the first two types. In this type, each phrase of the chorale is given an elaborate setting which is started before the chorale phrase makes its appearance. This setting usually makes use of the beginning of the phrase to be set, so that a pre-imitation of the melody of the chorale takes place. Example 111 (page 195) shows this technique. As is usual, the fragments of the chorale in the setting are in diminution to set them off from the melody of the chorale, which appears in long notes in the soprano voice. Sometimes this statement

of the chorale is played by a hand which has only the one part, so that it may be played on a different manual of the organ to gain a separate tone color.

This is one of the most elaborate forms of chorale prelude, and one that is most characteristic, since it provides an elaborate setting for the chorale and also an imitative treatment of it. Such a chorale prelude may provide long passages where the melody of the chorale is not present but which are devoted to the setting. Sometimes the setting has a melody of its own and is almost capable of standing alone. Notice how similar this is to the contemporary type of theme and variations illustrated by the example from the Stravinsky *Octet*.

CHORALE CANTATA

Chorale cantatas are similar to the other types of cantatas that were discussed in Chapter VI, except that they are based on a chorale. In the simplest case, the text of the chorale is used in its entirety, the text of each verse furnishing the words for a movement. The melody of the chorale in a simple or ornamented form is also used. Sometimes there is additional text inserted between verses of the chorale to amplify its meaning, and this forms the basis for recitatives and arias for soloists. One verse of the chorale, usually the last, may be presented in a simple four-part harmonization, and for this purpose a chorus is required. Since it would not be effective to use the chorus for only one number, a chorale cantata may have several large movements for chorus and orchestra in addition to those movements that feature the soloists. The cantata that is discussed here is representative of this type. The text of the chorale is three stanzas long, and additional text is inserted between each stanza, creating the solo and duet numbers.

Variation Forms   195

J. S. Bach: *Wachet auf, ruft uns die Stimme* (Sleepers, Wake)

This cantata consists of seven movements the first, fourth, and seventh of which are settings of the chorale melody and text. The first movement opens with an orchestral introduction, after which the sopranos enter with the melody of the chorale in long notes. The other three sections of the chorus and the orchestra provide an elaborate setting for this melody, much in the manner of the third type of chorale prelude, except that here the melodies of the setting are not drawn from the chorale. Since the melody of the chorale is to be the basis of several movements, it would be too repetitious to use it for all the settings of the chorale as well. Throughout this movement the melody of the chorale is always in the soprano part and is all that the sopranos sing; it is therefore easily identified. There are long passages in which the sopranos and the chorale melody are not present—these sometimes use the rest of the chorus and the orchestra, sometimes just the orchestra. In spite of these passages the overall form of the movement is dictated by the chorale, since the movement's whole purpose is to provide a setting for one verse of the chorale.

The second movement is a short recitative for the tenor soloist, after which the bride and bridegroom are realistically represented by a soprano and bass duet. This a good example of amplification of the text. The chorale refers to a bridegroom, and in this movement he is represented by the bass soloist. This duet is a typical ritornello form, the first ritornello being in C minor, the tonic key, and the others being in G minor, E flat major, and finally C minor again. As is to be expected, the ritornellos use only the orchestra.

The fourth movement is the best known in this cantata. Here only the tenor section is used, singing the chorale while the orchestra again furnishes a setting. In this case the setting contains an unusually expressive melody, and more than half the time this melody is heard without the chorale melody. Once again the setting for the chorale is more important and expressive than the chorale itself. Perhaps this is not quite the case, for since the purpose of the movement is to provide a setting for a verse of the chorale, the impressive setting can be viewed as an amplification of the expression of this verse. It is possible to make a comparison of this movement with the third type of chorale prelude, and in this case the comparison is well taken, for Bach himself made a very literal transcription of this movement for organ and published it as a chorale prelude, the first of the six in the *Schübler* collection. This set of chorale preludes consists entirely of transcriptions of cantata movements and illustrates how closely related are the uses of the chorale in organ and vocal music.

The sixth movement is again a duet for the soprano and bass soloists. Since the first duet was a ritornello form, this one uses the other common aria form of the Baroque Era, the large ternary form that makes use of a *da capo* to return the A section. The last movement is a straightforward four-part harmonization of the third verse of the chorale, the instruments simply doubling the voice parts. Thus the cantata ends with the simplest and most direct statement of the chorale on which it is based.

EXAMPLES FOR ANALYSIS

SEPARATE VARIATIONS

Beethoven: *Piano Sonata No. 10, Op. 14, No. 2—2nd Movement*

Brahms: *Variations on a Theme of Handel, Op. 24*

Brahms: *Variations on a Theme of Haydn, Op. 56A* (Orchestra) *or 56B* (Two Pianos)

Stravinsky: *Concerto per due Pianoforte Soli—3rd Movement, Quattro Variazioni*

CONTINUOUS VARIATIONS

Purcell: *Dido and Aeneas—No. 2, Ah! Belinda—No. 24, Oft She Visits—No. 37 When I am Laid in Earth*

Bach: *Partita No. 2 for Violin Solo—Chaconne*

Beethoven: *Thirty-two Variations in C Minor*

Brahms: *Symphony No. 4 in E Minor, Op. 98—Finale*

William Schuman: *Symphony No. 3—Passacaglia*

XI

Free Forms

THIS CHAPTER heading is something of a misnomer, since the pieces discussed here are not free in the sense of being very loosely constructed, but rather in the sense that their form is more nearly unique and therefore fits no general classification.

This book has been concerned in the main with a series of general formal patterns for pieces or movements of pieces. This has been true because the book is intended as an introduction to the subject of structure in music, and a consideration of these general formal types gives some organization to the subject. Composers themselves are free to construct any form they wish for a particular piece, but it is significant that most of the music written over the last several centuries makes use, at least to some degree, of one of the forms that have been presented. This shows to what extent composers themselves are influenced by the practices of music as they find it as young men, and to what extent these general formal designs exist for composers as very real entities. At the same time, if each new composer slavishly followed the formal patterns of the past, these forms would soon lose any expressive meaning for an audience too aware of the order of events in the form. So it is that each new composer must take the forms of the past and change and reshape them to suit his purpose. Sometimes no design within the composer's experience is suitable for the expression he seeks, and he is then impelled to create a completely new design to suit his purposes. If this design is successful the composer who created it or some other composer may use it, and if this happens enough a new form appears.

Such creation is often lost in the obscurity of the past, for basic innovations in form are not necessarily the work of those composers whom posterity ultimately judges to be the most expressive, and whose music survives their own time. Such basic formal innovations are obviously rare. Not many different formal patterns have been discussed in this book, in spite of the large literature of music; moreover, some of the forms studied have their origins in other forms that have been gradually modified. This means that most often when a composer feels compelled to create a more unique design for a piece, no other pieces quite like it appear, and it remains as a single example of its technique. In such a case the analyst faces a greater challenge—he must discover not only the design of the piece, but what it is that motivated it, and what it is that makes it effective. Perhaps the most significant advice that can be given for the analysis of such music is to say that the piece must be examined of itself. The design of one of the common forms must not be sought too strenuously, lest the analyst be blinded to the method of construction of the piece he is examining. This is true to an extent of any new piece or movement that is analyzed, but as we have seen certain formal procedures are typical of certain periods, performance media, and types of pieces, so that the analyst has a certain expectation of what form he will find when he looks at a new piece.

It is the purpose of this chapter to analyze several works that are in no way representative of the forms already studied. But while the four pieces discussed in this chapter are each unusual in form, the basic means used by composers to create form in a piece are used in these pieces just as in any others. Only occasionally, as in the *Fantasy* of Mozart, does an approach that considers the typical means of construction fail to explain the formal unity that can be felt. In such a case, further search is necessary, for, as in this example by Mozart, the strength and unity of a form that can be felt can be analyzed. If the Mozart analysis were read without reference to the music, the reader might well think that he was reading an analysis of some complex contemporary composition, for the general patterns of the forms of one's own era do not always seem clear. The organization of many contemporary pieces is often puzzling, but no doubt in time this organization will become clearer, and by the twenty-first century it will seem relatively simple, and students of form will be more puzzled by the music of their own time. It should be noticed that examples from contemporary pieces were studied throughout the book, and it was only in the study of theme and variations that contemporary practices had to be studied as a separate topic. The four examples analyzed in this chapter are not all contemporary, but rather come from the Baroque, Classic, Romantic, and Contemporary Eras. Each period has produced music of unusual design, and it should be remembered that certain general types of pieces, such as preludes, have been mentioned about which it was not possible to make a definite statement as to what formal design might be expected. The four analyses that follow differ in purpose from the others found in this book, in that they are not intended to illustrate a general musical form, but rather the analytical approach to pieces of unusual design.

J. S. Bach: *The Well–tempered Clavier, Vol. I—Prelude No. 3*

From its first to its last chord the motion of this prelude never stops or even slackens. Nonetheless, four distinct sections may be discovered, and the most unusual feature of the form of this work is the arrangement of the sections, not the continuous nature of the piece. Since the four sections are not separated by a pause or even a strong cadence, Bach separates them by the melodic material found in each. The first section extends from bar 1 through bar 31, the second from bar 32 through 46, the third from 47 through 62, and the last from bar 63 through 96, with the last eight bars serving as a coda. These main sections are separated by their melodic content, and a detailed consideration will show the exact content and structure of each.

The first section starts out with an eight-bar idea in the tonic key of C sharp major. In the ninth bar this idea is repeated in the dominant with the original two parts inverted. In bar 17 this tonal motion through the circle of fifths continues with the two parts in their original position in the two hands in the key of D sharp minor. This and the A sharp minor passage that follows continue the motion through the circle of fifths. However the minor mode is the mode that one would expect of the supertonic and submediant chords in C sharp major, thus retaining the suggestion that this whole section is really a very colorful harmonic progression in the tonic key of C sharp major. These four appearances of the opening idea constitute the entire first section.

The next section starts with a two-bar idea using eighth notes, including two eights that tie in the right hand and a two-bar sixteenth-note pattern in the left hand. These figures are repeated in sequence and then inverted for two appearances of the two patterns together. This whole procedure is then repeated to produce another eight bars. The forward motion in this section is increased by the tonal motion. The keys reached successively are E sharp minor, then down a second to D sharp minor, up a fifth to A sharp minor and down a second to G sharp major, up a fifth to D sharp minor and down a second to C sharp major, and finally up a fourth to F sharp major, the key of the next section. The tonic notes of each of these keys make a very obvious pattern, but the mode chosen in each case is that of the corresponding chords in the key of C sharp major, the tonic key of the entire prelude.

The third section returns the opening material, but at the start the sixteenth notes are in the left hand and the quarter and eighth notes are in the right hand. Again this is followed by the inversion of this pattern in the dominant key of F sharp, but this presents the two melodies in their original order and key, measures 55 and following being the same as the opening measures. After this the fourth section enters at once, and unlike the other three sections, which have changed key constantly, this last section is very static tonally. There are two distinct ideas in this section, one at the beginning and a second at bar 75, this latter with some tonal motion. At bar 87 the first of the ideas of this section returns an octave lower, so this section, unlike the others, is a rounded form. The brief coda that follows is freely constructed, based on arpeggios that provide a figuration of a strong harmonic progression.

Expressed in letters the plan of this movement would be A B A C, a plan that is strong as it is organized here, but one that is not typical. Several commonplace formal techniques can be seen in the work. The material of the opening is returned, but it is in the middle of the piece and in the subdominant key. There is a strong tonal arch, but the tonic key is reached some distance before the end of the piece, and the key remains essentially tonic from that point. Thus it is the actual use and arrangement of the formal materials that is unusual in this prelude, not the materials themselves.

Mozart: *Fantasia in C Minor, K. 475*

This fantasy is usually coupled with the *C Minor Piano Sonata* (K. 457) in performance, a practice evidently established by Mozart himself. A brief examination of the form of the fantasy discloses that it consists of a series of sections, each different from the others with the exception of the last section, which returns the material of the first. Not only are the sections quite unlike one another in mood, tempo, and theme, but several of them do not really come to a convincing ending, breaking off instead to yield to a new and totally different section. The analytical problem comes from the fact that when one becomes very well acquainted with the work, a feeling of a unity and structural organization arises that belies the fragmentary effect produced on first hearing. The first section extends from the beginning of the fantasy to the middle of the second page, ending just before the first repeated strain. The second section starts at that point and continues to the *Allegro*, at which point the third section starts. Immediately after the ending of the third section, section four starts at the *Andantino* and continues until that tempo is replaced by *Più allergo*. This is the start of the fifth section and it continues until the *Tempo primo* announces the return of the opening at the start of the sixth and last section. Expressed in letters this form would be A B C D E A. Furthermore, the fact that the tempo markings can be used to identify the start of each new section indicates how little successive sections are connected. Here then we have a work in which the usual methods are of little help in trying to determine the source of the unity of the form. The next approach is to make a detailed study and description, and from this seek the nature of the formal organization.

The first section starts with a C minor theme that is introduced in octaves and then extended by a treatment of the first bar in first the right hand and then the left. This leads to a new melodic idea in bar 18 which sounds like a closing theme and serves this purpose in this section, starting in G major, moving up a third to B minor, and then modulating at the last moment to D major for the start of the second section in bar 26. This second section is a ternary form with two repeated strains. The repeat of the second strain is written out, but can be clearly heard. The second time through the second strain is not complete. The music breaks off one bar short of the end, and after a hesitant repetition of a melodic figure, the next section bursts in.

The third section starts with a fast agitated them in A minor which is immediately repeated in G minor. This leads to a new theme in F major which is of a more lyric nature, although the excited mood of the start of this section is never quite lost. The key soon shifts from F major to F minor, and a series of a rapid modulations follows, so that it is difficult to assign any tonic key to this section. Except for this key pattern, the section sounds rather like the start of the exposition of a sonata form. The two themes are rather typical of a first and second theme, although the whole procedure disintegrates soon after the appearance of the second theme. Section Four is a binary form in B flat major, with the repeats of both parts written out. The binary form is of the sort seen so frequently in which there are implications of ternary form as well. Again a transition passage leads directly to a fast section, and this fifth section, like the third, is neither in a closed form nor tonally stable. Since it is based on a single motive, there is a suggestion of a development section, but a development of a figure that has not been used previously in the piece. The last section is clearly a return of the first, presenting the opening theme followed by the closing theme, both now in C minor, so that the fantasy ends in that key.

The structure of the form is now beginning to reveal itself. Of the six sections, the first and last are related, the second and fourth are related, and the third and fifth are related. The nature of these last two relationships was hinted at in the description of the fifth section. Both the third and fifth sections are fast and agitated, both are in open forms that have strong starts and inconclusive endings, and both sections are fluid tonally, passing so rapidly through successive keys that no single key stands out as the tonic key of the section. In a sense, then, the fifth section is just like the third, except that the themes of the third section are not present. In the same way the second and fourth sections are similar. Both are in closed forms, one binary and one ternary, both are slow and placid, and both have a single tonic key. Here is one of the most striking relationships in the fantasy, for the second section is in D major, the key a whole step above the tonic key of C minor, and the fourth section is in B flat major, a whole step below tonic. Since the third and fifth sections are in no definite key, the motion from C minor to D major to B flat major and then back to C minor is the basic tonal motion of the work, and a curiously modern tonal plan it is. The symmetry and perfection of this plan cannot be accidental, and Mozart's formal thinking can be seen to be far in advance of his time. If the similar sections were to be assigned the same letter, the scheme of the form would be A B C B C A, a very concise structure and the one that is felt when the fantasy is heard even before it is perceived intellectually.

The major task in this analysis was to find unity among diverse sections, but when the common unities of theme and key were sought no relationships were at first found. Further examination did at last yield relationships between the sections which, while they are unconventional, are as strong as those more commonly used. The key to the analysis of such a work is to discover the true nature of the piece being considered, rather than to look for confirmation of an expectation or a guess.

Wagner: *Siegfried Idyll*

The themes of the *Siegfried Idyll* are from Wagner's cycle of music dramas, *The Ring of the Nibelung*. But although they are readily identified with their source in the operas, such identification is not germane to the form of the work. As is often the case with a work where the themes are from another work and where the use of the themes is the object of the piece, there is a formal organization to this work, and one that is effective even if the listener has no prior acquaintance with the themes. Thus we can consider the form of this piece without reference to the use and meaning of the themes in the operas.

The themes chosen by Wagner for inclusion in this work evidently did not suggest some common form, for the design of this piece is unique. This is not to say that all the procedures of the piece are new, for there is a heavy influence of sonata form, but the actual details of the design are not those usually found in this or any other form. There are five basic sections to the work, the last being a recapitulation of the first. Beyond this there is no thematic relationship between the sections, although in two places themes from one section are heard in another.

The work starts with an introduction based on the main theme of the work. This theme is first hinted at and then gradually presented more clearly and in a more complete form. The first complete statement comes in the first violin in bar 29, and two bars later a second part of the theme is found in the woodwinds. This is gradually amplified until a climax is reached at bar 48, after which the music dies away quickly and moves rapidly to the key of B major, which is reached in bar 55 with a melody derived from the principal theme. A closing theme follows, which is introduced rather tentatively by the strings in bar 63 and then passed to the woodwinds. Further subsidiary climaxes are reached, but this section gradually dies away after the closing theme has been reached, and at bar 91 a new theme in the oboe marks the beginning of the second section. This section starts in B major, the key of the closing theme of the previous section. The new theme in the oboe is next developed, after which there are two statements of the principal theme from the first section with the theme of this section in counterpoint. These come at bar 109 in the key of B major and at bar 116 on the tonic key of E major. After this the section dies away and quickly comes to an end in bar 125.

There follows a transition section based on the theme of the second section in G major. Although it is not a part of the section on either side, it serves to bridge the shift of mood from the second to the third section. The third section starts in bar 148, and two bars later the clarinet introduces the main theme of this section. This is passed from instrument to instrument and greatly developed in a manner suggestive of sonata form. The section starts in A flat major, but in bar 194 there is a dramatic shift to A major which, in turn, leads to the key of B major, and in bar 201 the theme of the third section is used in counterpoint with a return of the principal theme from the first section. This theme has been rhythmically altered to fit the three-four meter of this section, but it is clearly recognizable, since it is played by the oboe. These two themes are heard together again in bar 218 in the key of A flat, the tonic key of this section, and then the theme of the third section is further developed alone, shifting through several keys. There is a build-up to a forceful climax which is reached in bar 255, but this climax suddenly breaks off, and swirling descending triplets in the violins and flute lead directly to the horn solo that begins the next section.

As was the case at the beginning of the previous two sections, the fourth section starts with a new theme and a completely new mood. Wagner was obviously interested in delineating the several sections of this work. The key of this section is C major, and after the horn call and attendant bird calls in the woodwinds, there is another buildup, this time to bar 286 where the principal theme from the first section is recapitulated in the tonic key of E major. Admittedly the fourth section is short, and in some ways is more an introduction to the recapitulation than a separate section. The basis for calling it a separate section is that both a new theme and a new key are introduced, and these seem sufficient reasons to suggest an independent section. The mood of the principal theme is much different at bar 286, since the previous excitement remains, and the passage that follows the recapitulation is the climax of the entire piece. The key of C returns vigorously at bar 296 and a final climax in F comes in bar 306. There is a sudden drop to a soft dynamic level, and the closing material from the first section follows (bar 308). The only basic difference is that, as is true in a sonata form, the closing theme is now centered in the tonic key of E major, instead of in the dominant key that was used before.

In bar 351 the principal theme returns in the complete form that was first heard in bar 29, and again the second part of it is in the clarinet. It is a moot point whether this is the start of a coda or whether the coda comes at the *Molto tranquillo* in bar 366. At this later point the themes of the fourth section (horn call and bird sounds) and second section are quoted in a fragmentary fashion, after which the movement gradually dies away to the end. Once more before the piece ends the principal theme is heard.

This principal theme dominates the entire work, since it forms the basis for the first and fifth sections and is heard in the second and third in counterpoint with the main themes of those two sections. The work has an interesting key pattern, since basically the first and fifth sections are in the tonic key, the second section is in the dominant key, and the third and fourth sections are in the two major keys a third above and below the tonic key, A flat major and C major, respectively. The whole work exhibits a tightness of design that one would not suspect in any piece that gathers together themes from another work. The form that seems to have most influenced Wagner when he was composing this piece is sonata form, but no light is shed on the piece by asserting that it *is* a sonata form, since its actual form is closer to the unique than to the sonata.

Bartók: *Sonata for Piano—Finale*

This movement poses the opposite problem from that of the Mozart fantasy considered earlier, for in the fantasy there are a profusion of themes, while in this movement there seems at first to be but one important theme. This theme is presented at the beginning, and the entire movement seems like a long development of it. Actually this is not true, since three different ideas can be identified, but an examination of them will reveal problems in naming them. The movement opens with a theme that in a sonata form would certainly be called first theme. At bar 20 a new melodic idea appears that complements the first theme and answers it, and again, if this were a sonata form, this new theme would be called first theme, part two. The problem is that these two melodic ideas, which come together like the two parts of a single theme, are actually the basic melodic materials for the entire piece. This would suggest calling them first and second theme, but only if it is clearly understood that they are not differentiated to the extent that the two themes of a sonata form are, nor are they separated in space as are the themes of a sonata form. At bar 38 there is another new idea that is of formal significance and, for the purposes of this discussion, this can be called third theme. An alternative nomenclature might be to speak of first, second, and third idea, or themes A, B, and C, but these labels are really no more descriptive of the function of these melodic ideas in this piece than are the terms chosen.

The first theme, which is found at the beginning of the movement, is subjected to many transformations in the course of the movement, but its essential nature is always clearly recognizable. The same is not always true for the second theme that appears in bar 20, and it is necessary to consider the most essential feature of this theme so that its return will be apparent. The basis of this theme is the series of eighth notes that rises to one or two quarter notes. At measure 26 this feature of the second theme is the basis for an imitative passage in which the beginning of the theme is suggested by the left hand and its inversion by the right hand. This leads to a climactic passage in bar 38 which is Theme Three. This theme disintegrates into a passage at bar 49 that serves as a setting for the second appearance of the first theme, which is repeated several times each time with some alteration, the most striking change being the elongation of the last note of the phrase. Bar 84 is suggestive of the third theme, but the first theme soon returns at bar 92 to be developed a new way. At bar 111 the second theme returns for an extended treatment that includes considerable inversion. This is then followed by two more treatments of the first theme, one beginning in bar 143 and the other in bar 157. In bar 169 the scale lines suggest the treatment of the second theme first found in bar 26. This leads to a return of the second theme in bar 175 that is so literal that it sounds like a recapitulation. The passage following this exactly parallels the imitative passage from the first presentation of this theme and reaches the third theme in bar 192 in the original fashion. Once more the first theme returns for further development, several different treatments of the theme being identifiable. These start in bars 205 and 227, with a suggestion of Theme Three starting in bar 217. The movement ends with one final climax on the material of the third theme.

A designation of the parts of this form by letter would shed little light on it since there is a constant alternation of the three themes rather than an organization into large sections. Although the three themes return so many times, they are so changed in melody or setting that they never become tiring. The first theme dominates the entire movement. On becoming familiar with the movement, one begins to suspect that the ideas that are called Theme Two and Theme Three are really derived from the first theme, in which case the movement is truly monothematic. In any case, the form is very intense and highly unified, and it may be that Bartók used this form instead of sonata form because the latter was not tightly knit enough for his purposes in this movement.

In the same fashion any piece, however complex, may be found to have a strongly organized form. The analyses in this chapter are intended to serve as models for the analysis of atypical works. In a sense they do, since they make the basic point that whatever it is that contributes to the structure of a piece must be considered in the analysis. In another sense, these analyses are of less help than those earlier in the book, since the works discussed here are so unusual that a knowledge of them cannot be applied to any other work. However, although these compositions are more unusual in form, they are not necessarily weaker than pieces that use the common forms studied in earlier chapters.

Conclusion

MOST OF THIS book has been devoted to basic formal patterns in common use during the last three hundred years. The various forms have been described in terms sufficiently general to embrace much of the music written during this period, and therefore no form has been studied in sufficient detail to cover all the possibilities for its use or the many variants that composers have fashioned from it. These can be studied only by examining many examples of each form from many different composers, performance media, and historical eras. When many variants of these forms have been studied it will be found that the system of classifying forms used in this book is only relatively true. Since any system of classification must be based on the literature of music, such a system is bound to contain ambiguities and contradictions due to the endless variety of structures that composers devise. It should always be remembered that whatever system of classification is used, the great composers of the past were under no obligation to provide clear-cut examples of it, nor is the ease of classifying the form of a piece of music a measure of its formal strength.

The vastness of the literature makes a study of form in music arduous but rewarding. This vastness also helps to explain many seeming contradictions in various studies of the subject; these contradictions cause less and less vexation as the literature of music is studied further. It is especially important to study many and varied examples from the twentieth century. As time passes, the basic patterns of form used in this century will become apparent, and one day our century will seem as clear to the students of form as those of the past seem to us.

Index